REFLECTIONS
on the
UNKNOWABLE

REFLECTIONS
on the
UNKNOWABLE

Thomas Keating

LANTERN BOOKS ✦ NEW YORK

A Division of Booklight Inc.

2014

Lantern Books

128 Second Place

Brooklyn, NY 11231

www.lanternbooks.com

All Biblical quotations are from the New Revised Standard
Version of the Bible copyright © 1989 by the Division of Christian
Education of the National Council of Churches
of Christ in the United States of America.

Cover photograph by W.T. Bryant

Library of Congress Cataloging-in-Publication Data

Keating, Thomas.
Reflections on the unknowable / Thomas Keating.
pages cm
Includes bibliographical references.
ISBN 978-1-59056-437-0 (pbk. : alk. paper)—
ISBN 978-1-59056-438-7 (ebook)
1. Spirituality—Catholic Church—Meditations.
2. Spiritual life—Catholic Church—Meditations.
3. Contemplation—Meditations. I. Title.
BX2350.65.K43 2014
242—dc23
2013042393

CONTENTS

Special thanks to
Bonnie Shimizu for her editorial help.

PART I

AN
INTERVIEW
WITH
THOMAS
KEATING

AN INTERVIEW WITH
THOMAS KEATING

The following interview was conducted on January 19, 2013, by Rick Archer on the show "Buddha at the Gas Pump," which interviews spiritual practitioners on the religious life. The interview has been edited for clarity and precision and to remove false starts, hesitations, and repetitions. You can view the whole interview at http://batgap.com/thomas-keating/—Ed.

RICK ARCHER (RA): I would like to start by asking you some very fundamental questions, maybe even metaphysical. Then we could move on to your idea of the road map of the territory from initial awakening to spiritual interest to its culmination, and then we can talk about centering prayer and contemplative prayer.

Let me start with the most fundamental question. In reading your books, the word "God" is mentioned many, many times. So please define what you understand or experience God to be. What is God?

TK: This is a difficult term in interreligious dialogue, because there are as many ideas of God as there are people. "God" was used originally in the Hebrew Bible in distinction to the other local gods of different city states. It was not even a national deity, but people looked to some entity, some higher power, to protect them from their enemies. It would be nicer if we had another word for God. But one can avoid getting too metaphysical and just quote the Hebrew Bible, "I am who I am" or "I am *that* I am" [Exodus 3:14]—a text discussed at length by many scripture scholars.

Thus, the best description of God is "is-ness" without any limit: "I am" without any other pronoun. The Buddhists have done well in establishing an attitude towards the uncreated God as distinct from the God of creation or the creator God. It's the same God, of course, but God as I will use the term here is simply a label. It is the one I'm used to in my tradition. Maybe someone can invent a better one. God is everything. Call him "Butch" if you'd like!

RA: There's a tussle that's been going on between science and religion for quite some time. When I look at anything of a scientific nature, or if I look at a presentation on astronomy, for instance or a Discovery Channel show about the microscopic world, or listen to a quantum physicist, to me I am hearing and seeing God. That's what they are talking about: this incredible explosive. Infinite creativity is micromanaging every subatomic particle and yet, at the same time, managing the galaxies.

TK: You have certainly got the right idea as far as a Christian perspective, especially that of the mystics. But, of course, one's idea of God changes as one's own consciousness matures and one gives up treating God as a kind of dependency where one may get into codependent attitudes or even demanding attitudes towards God. The main thing is to have a big idea of God—huge! Science, both the infinitesimal aspect of it and the grandiose astronomical aspect of it, are presenting us with a new cosmology that religion has to take into account, especially the Christian tradition. Our scriptures are really based on a view of God that is patriarchal and limited by the culture of the time, and it just doesn't work anymore. Theology needs a solid cosmology on which to build a theology that will appeal to people of our time.

RA: Would you be comfortable in using the "omni" adjectives for God: omnipresent, omniscient, omnipotent? Does that jive with your experience of God or intuitive sense of God?

TK: Yes, but they're a little too metaphysical. They come from the essentialist metaphysics of the Middle Ages, which was a great tool of research and did a good job for its time, but has severe limitations because God has aspects that are beyond reason. Those aspects don't reject reason, but reason isn't enough. For instance, how do you resolve infinite justice and infinite mercy? You don't on the rational level. It remains a mystery, a contradiction. You have to open your consciousness and transcend the rational concept of God. It's only in the experience of that transcendent presence that one perceives that God is in everything without being limited to anything. God is as dynamic and expansive as change itself, and that is what is changeless about him.

The dynamic idea of God that evolutionary cosmology has provided for us (and only in the past fifty years in a convincing way) is a revelation of a higher power in which we are immersed and engulfed, and can never be separated from, because we have really no identity except what has emerged in the evolutionary process. Creation is not a one-time event. It's always happening, and in a sense, the being of God is always becoming. Becoming what? Becoming everything. Human consciousness is really God experiencing human consciousness. That means that we're a kind of icon of God, as Bernard Lonergan put it. This is why humans are so important. God dwells in them and is calling them into a certain equality as far as that's possible, given the fact that humans have limitations even after they have been healed by the infinite gifts of the Almighty and Merciful One.

Whatever we say of God we have to be prepared to say the opposite. He doesn't quite fit into any affirmative statements. If you say "he is . . ." you have to be willing to say "he isn't. . . ." He isn't anybody you can think of, that's for sure. Thus, one of the main breakthroughs of the spiritual journey is to perceive that God is manifesting in us and inviting us to become fully human because that is the way to become as fully divine as humans can be in this evolutionary process. We don't know the end, but there's no reason that the process should stop. We've been evolving from amoebas for several billions of years and we haven't stopped. The brain is still evolving, without question.

RA: I have a friend who likes to refer to us as sense organs of the Infinite. By that token, and if we consider God to be omnipresent, then not only are we sense organs of the Infinite but dogs and mosquitoes are, and even rocks, we could say. Everything expresses or reflects that to the best of its ability in terms of its physical structure.

TK: All that is congenial to my way of thinking. In regards to the development of consciousness from the infant, everyone starts out with almost zero self-consciousness, and begins to build a self that is dependent on parents, teachers, and its culture, along with its experience, temperament, and limitations. The world that we see, and that we are judging all the time, is very prejudiced. We see it through our tinted glasses. In that sense, the world is unreal—not because it *is* unreal, but because our *view* of it is. It is built on our desires of what we want it to be and our appetite for control, pleasure, and security. The spiritual life involves recognizing these appetites as illusions of our false self and detaching ourselves from them, without expecting that these problems are going to go away or that suffering is going to disappear. The spiritual life is precisely to lead this divine life in human circumstances that involve both suffering and great joy, and which is continuing to evolve. We don't know where it's going. We have to learn to take responsibility for the world that we are in. And this we are reluctant to do because it limits some of our desired freedoms.

RA: So, ultimately, when you get right down to it, we are God looking out through these eyes. You hinted that if you go to our very core, that's who and what we are. To what extent can that be realized? And if it is realized fully, say in the person of someone like Jesus Christ, does one actually rise above the possibility of suffering? From the perspective of suffering, people looked at Jesus and said, "Oh, he must be suffering terribly!" From his perspective, was he really suffering if he was fully one with God; or was he residing in a sort of a transcendent haven that was beyond anything his physical body was being subjected to?

TK: It's very important to understand suffering. Most of us are too busy getting away from our own personal suffering to think about it too much, unless we are thrust into or immersed in terrible suffering, as many people are today. This is where cosmology comes in. What does evolution mean? Does it mean that we are going to evolve out of suffering altogether while still in this life? That is not the promise. The promise is that we are developing our capacity as human beings to do the things that God does with the greatest of ease: to forgive, to show compassion, to respect everyone, and to experience oneness with everyone.

In the Christian perspective, God has identified with human nature in its spiritual poverty, sinfulness, and alienation from himself. That says so much about God. Why would God want to identify with such a helpless and spiritually destitute group of people, who are the lowest intellectual beings we know of in the universe? We may improve in the future, but right now we are pretty childish in many of our social choices.

God doesn't look at suffering the way we do. There is a deep interrelatedness among the Christian mysteries. The Trinity is *the* great mystery. Somehow God is a community. God is not three persons, as we understand "persons," but there are three relationships in God that treat us in a personal way.

God seems to adjust himself to every creature at its level

of consciousness, however primitive. What Jesus has done is to integrate the human condition with all its limitations. He completely identified with us as a human being. He threw away all the divine privileges and showed us how to be human in a divine way, which involves the realization of being called to unity with God and oneness with each other.

That seems to be the program: to change what is most opposite to God or distant and alienated from God into divine love itself, and in this way to manifest what is the deepest reality of God, which is his humility. He doesn't seem to care about being God. He has everything and has need of nothing, except to pour out his goodness and love on those who are willing to accept them. Once humans have a certain choice, limited though it is, God does not control everything that happens. He has to respect the gift he has given us of a significant degree of freedom and autonomy.

RA: It's reminiscent of an adolescent maturing into adulthood. At a certain point, the parent has to grant them a certain degree of autonomy and freedom. It's a very risky business and they might go off and do crazy things. But if that freedom isn't granted, they will never grow into adults.

TK: I agree. Parents need to trust children even when they make mistakes, because everybody makes mistakes in this society. Making mistakes is human, and God is not put off by it. There are trillions of chances and no lack of generosity or abundance on God's part.

RA: This discussion points to something that I find fascinating. I tried to write out a question to really express it clearly. So I'll just read it and maybe we can make sense of it: "Is loss of wholeness a necessary condition for manifestation? If somehow all the parts maintain full awareness of their essential nature as wholeness, it seems there wouldn't be any impetus for diversification. The tendency would be to merge back into wholeness, and actually some enlightened people have reflected this. They practically have to be fed to be kept alive, while others have become more dynamic and engaged in the world." . . .

I don't know if that was clear. But if you imagine the Big Bang and the manifestation of the universe, it almost seems that God necessarily has to play a hide-and-seek game with himself, where he creates these parts and appears to get lost in them, even though he essentially *is* the parts.

TK: What do you do if you are infinite and enjoy infinite happiness and don't need anything? What do you do to occupy yourself?

RA: You get bored. You say, "Hey, let's have some fun."

TK: Then what do you do?

RA: "Let's play. Let's create something."

TK: You play. In other words, there is a playful character to God. He wants to see what these creatures can do in different circumstances, and this enables him, by his identification with us, to experience what it's like to be human with our limitations: to love us in our weakness and spiritual poverty, and to enjoy healing and forgiving us. The things we find hard to do are what make God happiest.

RA: I came across a quote from Teresa of Avila. She said, "It appears that even God is on the journey." In other words, this whole process of the universe is one big evolutionary machine, which is God's spiritual practice.

TK: You hit the nail on the head when you said God likes to play hide and seek. That's the classical game. But that doesn't mean that he wants to cause us suffering. There is so much to learn, and one of the great things to learn is that the game of life is designed for us to enjoy fun, not to accomplish something. As soon as you want to win, you've lost the pleasure of playing. A certain amount of competition is not bad, but the fun is over once you make the game a career.

There are lots of games that God plays and another one he seems to like very much is, "Let's pretend." Or, "Let's do it again," like a child who finds great joy in knocking down a stack of blocks and then cries out, "Oh Daddy, let's do it again!" God also can play rough. He wants to see if we are willing to join him in the game. The most serious of games is that of healing the wounds of the world and becoming whole, which is the same idea as salvation or redemption. We are aware of having a capacity for boundless happiness. That may be the greatest proof of God's presence in us. Even in strange ways, people are always looking for happiness. If they are malicious, that's their idea of happiness.

RA: Like you said earlier, our perception of reality gets filtered through the lenses of our perception and becomes quite distorted in the process, at least at certain stages of our development. We think it is going to make us happy to kill somebody or rob a bank and things like that.

You mentioned a minute ago that God likes to play rough sometimes. There are probably inhabited planets throughout this vast universe that are routinely smashed to smithereens by asteroids, and this planet alone is evidence enough that all kinds of horrible things can happen. Thinkers and philosophers have pondered this phenomenon for millennia, and there have been books like *Why Do Bad Things Happen to Good People?*

Let me hear your comment on this thought. Would it have been possible for God to have set us in a universe that didn't have polarities? It seems the very nature of relativity is if you are going to have hot, you have to have cold. If you are going to have fast, you're going to have to have slow. If you're going to have happiness, you have to have suffering.

TK: That is the human condition. That's the way we were launched on our evolutionary process towards wholeness, not a possession of wholeness from the beginning that we could recognize. I think it is a good idea to remember that once God creates anything, he's in big trouble because it's not going to be God if it is a creature. It doesn't have the divine power. In creating creatures to share his happiness, he's taking the long view of reality that it's not going to be hunky-dory all the time. Certain situations have to evolve for people to be able to accept God, especially when he plays rough.

RA: If it is all about play . . .

TK: Not all about play. An aspect of reality is its playful side. Life on earth is a serious situation. It is also true that God has a great sense of humor and likes to play, and would like us to understand that some things he does are a game and not to be taken too seriously. Once you have creatures with free will, anything can happen, and perhaps that's why God made creation this way.

The Father, in the Trinitarian relationships, is infinite possibilities and the Son is the articulation of those possibilities in actuality. The Spirit is the complete surrender of the Father and the Son to each other in total oneness. God is infinitely one and infinitely diverse at the same time. The relationships in the Trinity couldn't be more different. The Father and the Son can never be made into one on every level. There are relationships in God that are distinct.

We're invited into this dynamic of self-giving love and this is a problem for us. Humans don't like being creatures. They want to be in control. They want to be in charge of their efforts and draw attention to themselves, which is not what God does. He just *is*. He doesn't need any attention and he doesn't need adulation. We need to remember that we are created out of nothing. As soon as we can fully accept that, and I emphasize *fully*, we can become everything. We can be God, too.

God, of course, can't support something that is not true. We are not God by nature, but we are invited to become God by grace, which is the sheer gratuity of God sharing his goodness, compassion, forgiveness, and oneness.

These are the real values of the human person. We're just barely beginning to emerge from the domination of our animal instincts. Some anthropologists think that the evolutionary process is at a critical point in our time, in which a new level of consciousness beyond the rational, the capacity to understand reality intuitively, may be beginning to emerge. The globalization of the world may be an opportunity in which the higher power can reveal to people at the same time insights into ultimate reality that we haven't been able to reach on the rational level and can't because of the limitations of that level of consciousness.

RA: Someone once brought up the metaphor to me that two thousand years ago, in the time of Christ and Buddha, it was as if there was a very thick membrane that had to be penetrated in order to realize God and to become enlightened. But now that membrane has been penetrated over and over again so many times that it's become quite porous, and the price of entry is much lower now. People are having all these awakenings all over the place quite spontaneously, even without doing any spiritual practice—at least that they can remember.

TK: Yes. It's interesting that many people who can reasonably be believed about their spiritual experience are pointing to invisible energy that science hasn't taken into its reckoning as yet, and which it needs to do because of the increasing evidence that such energy exists. What holds the body together? There are trillions of cells with no apparent head office or center of activity, so that consciousness is a communion of all the possibilities of body, mind, and spirit, a kind of synthesis of all levels of creation. The human as "an icon of God" is worth reflecting upon.

If we try to dissolve difficulties on the rational level, we just get into emotional turmoil. To accept them, sit with them, wait them out, and give them to God is the best way to deal with suffering, according to the mystics of the world traditions.

RA: And perhaps to learn to embrace paradox and to encompass irreconcilable notions within one's noggin.

TK: Yes. This is why meditation is so important. It's probably the most direct access to our capacities for consciousness beyond the rational level. One of the great and timeless questions is, "Who are you?" Adolescents are said to take great interest in that question. Who we are is certainly not in our résumé or what you tell a doctor about your medical history. It's not about personality and character as expressed in our behavior and way of looking at the world.

Beyond the egoic self, as it's usually called, is a self that we don't normally access except through meditation, prayer, or some special invasion of God's presence in our life. At the deepest level, there is a self even beyond the true self, and this is the manifestation of God in our spiritual poverty and weakness. Somehow, who God is is expressed in the experience of human weakness.

In meditation, by sitting long enough, the dust begins to settle and you begin to see more clearly that the deepest self is God-consciousness manifested in our uniqueness as human beings. We are completely united with everyone else in the human species because God is in everyone else. To me, this is one of the great gifts of evolutionary cosmology and of science today and why religion has to listen to science. It's giving us up-to-date revelations of who God is and developing a cosmology that can support deep union with God.

What is being revealed is that everything is interconnected and interrelated in the material universe and functions in collaboration and communion with other creatures. As you go up the levels of consciousness, the presence and action of God are in everything that happens: not just God's presence, but God's presence *and action*. That action is healing the conscious and unconscious wounds of growing up and childhood trauma, and at the same time activating all the capacities of grace—which are, in the Christian scheme of things, the fruits and gifts of the Spirit. In this perspective, death is not the end. It is the completion of the human journey that prepares us to move beyond human support systems and all forms of possessiveness, just to be who we are and to be content and happy with that immense gift.

RA: Death is just a pit stop. I know this is not part of the official Christian doctrine, but do you personally believe in reincarnation? Do you feel that the soul carries on from life to life and evolves in that way? Or does that not fit for you?

TK: It doesn't appeal to me, at least from my experience. People seem to have past-life experiences that are very strong. We know now that every experience is recorded in our bodies somewhere, and maybe there's some master database, where everything that has ever happened is recorded. In this view nothing dies except what is false. And you don't have to wait to die physically to die to the illusion of the false self.

RA: Are you saying that when you have a past-life experience you're picking up on somebody else's memory that was recorded in the cosmic computer?

TK: I'm saying it could be possible because of the oneness of human nature. We think past-life experiences are our own, but they might not be. In actual fact, I don't know, and so I'm happy to respect the fact that so many people believe in reincarnation. Actually, I think both could be possible.

RA: It's just that the vast majority of humanity obviously did not end up at the pinnacle of human spiritual evolution. So what happens to them? Do they get another chance, or what?

TK: That's the great question! I don't think you will ever get a completely satisfying answer. It doesn't matter what happens, as long as it's God's will. God's will is one of infinite love and compassion and is trying to initiate us into our particular contribution to the evolutionary process. We can't do that without a community; that is, without support from other folks and learning from others. We need the support, the encouragement, the trust, the love of a community to become fully human.

There is a lot of interesting information about dying nowadays. Actually, many hospice people are beginning to say that the dying process is a transformative process. As the dying go through the stages that Elisabeth Kübler-Ross identified, one moves from denial to anger to fear to acceptance to peace to joy.

RA: If death is gradual, I suppose you could do that.

TK: God isn't limited by time, so he can transform us in a nanosecond. But it's a good question. In other words, we are always looking at reality or the biggest events from our limited perspective, with our tinted glasses from what we heard in kindergarten, from our parents, or from important others. We have to graduate from those attitudes or at least re-evaluate them, which most people do in adolescence and early adulthood.

We need to provide young people with opportunities to

discuss these basic issues of life, more than they seem to have in most universities today. There is a preoccupation with drink and sex. That is the way it was when I was in college and that's the way it still is. It's childish, but it's a way of growing into one's own decision-making capacities. Young people need to be loved by parents in that state of uncertainty. We've all made more or less the same mistakes. And we will not recover by means of advice alone, but only from being loved in our mistakes.

RA: You've mentioned the false self several times. Perhaps we should get into that. In your books, you outline in great detail how the false self gets formed and how eventually it is seen through. In contemporary spiritual circles there seems to be a lot of talk of "no self," there being no one home, so to speak, and of being egoless. It would be interesting to discuss this for a few minutes.

TK: There are some very good books on the subject. Thomas Merton has one from a contemplative perspective [*What Is Contemplation?*]. We have to take steps as we grow conscious of the self to protect the life that we have. The false self is a project to build a self out of what we perceive in early childhood to be sources of happiness or gratification. Security symbols, affection and esteem symbols, and the desire for control and power, are normal instincts necessary for survival in infancy.

But since there are no standards to judge these attractions, they tend to become not just needs, but demands. Since everybody else has the same needs and demands, we're in for social conflict. Here is where an appropriate religious instruction could be extremely helpful in preparing the human psyche for maturation and going beyond. The gratification of those three energy centers, when excessive, produces inevitable frustration. Then come the afflictive emotions, like anger and grief, and you are in various negative moods for hours, days, years, or a lifetime. The false self doesn't exist. It's all in our heads.

RA: It sounds like you're saying that even though ultimately the false self doesn't exist, it's necessary to form one in order to function as a human being. Would it be possible for a child to grow and not form one at all?

TK: It might be better to call that the *ego*. Ego is the expansion of the necessary human values that are involved in development. It's the exaggeration of them, the fixation on them, or the addictive process that the false self initiates, that leads to exaggeration and frustration. These instincts are impossible to realize because everyone else is trying to do the same foolish thing—that is, squeezing gratification out of sense information that is meant to give pleasure, but can't give permanent pleasure or true happiness.

RA: In your experience, have you ever seen an example of anyone who has gone through infancy and adolescence and formed a healthy functional and necessary ego without forming what you call a false self?

TK: No, I haven't. The information that I would consider essential for human growth is missing in ordinary education. There is great care nowadays not to impose a religious attitude on children, which is perhaps correct. There's no universal set of ethical values that you can present to a child that would help it to see the values of moderation in its desires and openness to relationships with people we don't like, or at least genuine openness with people who are different from us.

RA: So are you saying that the absence of proper ethical training is the main culprit in the development of a false self and the fact that it is so predominant in our society?

TK: I think you need some basic ethics. But here's the problem. We don't have a common ethic among the world religions or no religions. His Holiness the Dalai Lama in his book *Beyond Religion* and in his activities in recent years, is trying to develop an ethic that is built on human nature and that everybody could identify with.

RA: And no religion would have a problem with, presumably.

TK: Yes. It would have to consist of very general principles, and then each religion could add the particularities that are special to their respective traditions. His Holiness had two main principles when I last heard him speak. One was the unity of the human family. If we could just believe the discoveries of science, which in microbiology and other sciences show how unified the development and structures of the living body are, we might be able, just from the facts of science, to realize that humans are inseparable from one another. Once you accept oneness as a principle of inter-human relationships, you feel responsible for everyone else's needs and sufferings. Most people are not about to take that on, unless they are strongly motivated.

RA: No man is an island.

TK: Exactly. If I'm suffering, everyone else is touched by this. As one of the quantum mechanic scientists said, "You can't have a thought without influencing everything in the universe instantaneously." Even a thought about others or a judgment of others, affects society in ways that we don't understand yet, or we don't realize the damage that negative thinking can produce. And especially negative acting out, like vengeance. No good has ever come from violence that has any permanency to it. Yet that's the regression that most humans go through in conflict situations; they regress to the level of their animal ancestors, which is to handle opposition or conflict with violence.

The evolutionary process is stuck or stalled at a point in which we can't go back to the irresponsibility of our animal ancestry, and we can't go forward into divine union without the grace of God. We are literally crucified between heaven and earth. When you look at a cross, even though nobody's on it, you see a marvelous symbol of where the human condition is right now. To get out of that place requires an integration of joy and sorrow, of hope and knowledge of our weakness. It is not just one thing, but the holistic development of all the human qualities that are inspired by principles that most people can accept. We can hope that science can convince us that we really are part of the oneness of everything and that what happens to one person affects us all. Saint Paul in his teaching on the mystical body of Christ expresses that insight from a spiritual perspective. We are mutually intended to support each other, and everyone is needed for the full health and development of the corporate body that is evolving through the liberation of the human family from its faults and limitations. The potential for the unity of the human family with God must be emphasized in every aspect of life, both private and societal.

RA: We were talking about how some sort of universal ethical training might prevent people from developing the false self, which causes so much trouble. I was thinking that maybe that's a top–down solution and that, in fact, your solution, which has been centering prayer, might get more to the root of the issue. In other words, ethical behavior might spontaneously spring from a deeper communion with God and with the innermost self, and that would take care of the issue. Some sort of universal training at an early age in something like centering prayer, contemplative prayer, might really transform society. I'm sure you've had that thought.

TK: Yes. I've had that thought. To be realistic, however, a number of people will think, "It comes from the Christian tradition and I'm not a Christian." Or some Christians who are very literal-minded will think, "This is not the way I understand the Bible."

RA: But you yourself have had an eclectic background with regard to meditation. I know you were exposed to Transcendental Meditation back in the 1970s. Would you agree that perhaps centering prayer could be adapted to any tradition and that within the context of every tradition something like centering prayer could be taught that would be harmonious with that religion?

TK: Sure. Some of the other major religions already have similar traditions and teachings. Centering prayer is a lot like zazen and the Buddhist Vajrayana practice.

RA: It's a lot like Transcendental Meditation, too.

TK: Vipassana is a concentrative process to control the mind. Centering prayer is a receptive practice. Anybody who can be receptive will benefit from it, and it could be presented or adapted to people without a particular religion. We've taught it in prisons, and there we discovered that when men in the yard saw their friends becoming more calm and peaceful, they asked what the cause was. Some asked to come to the weekly meetings, which was all the authorities would grant. Sometimes there was a lock-down and they couldn't get there.

In any case, those men who had no religion at all and who came to the weekly meetings began to experience the same effects of calm and less impulsive reactions to insults and negative situations. In other words, they were becoming more human. But you can't persuade people to do this; you can only offer it. There are a number of efforts being made, not only in centering prayer practice, but by other forms of meditation like the World Community for Christian Meditation founded by the Benedictine monk Dom John Main and spread around the world by Father Laurence Freeman, also a Benedictine monk.

RA: So what is centering prayer? How does it work?

TK: It doesn't "work." It is a receptive process.

RA: Describe the mechanics, if you will.

TK: We offer four guidelines. The first is to make the intention of consenting to God's presence and action within us. By "action," as I said earlier, we mean purification and the enhancement of spiritual practice: that is, the practice of the virtues of forgiveness, understanding, and the service of human needs. A lot depends on intention, so whenever you sit down to do the prayer, this is the first thing to do: resume your intention to consent. Consent is an enhanced form of acceptance. Acceptance is the necessary basic relationship with God, and consent is a little more personal and more warm. It is the *welcoming* of God's presence.

RA: Let's say you're teaching me centering prayer right now, and you're going to tell me to sit down and to have the attitude of relinquishing control: to consent, to be willing, malleable, receptive.

TK: Give yourself to God and put yourself in God's hands. Fall into the hands of the living God, so to speak. It's the safest place there is in all creation.

RA: It's not like, "I'm going to sit here and I'm going to do this, by golly!"

TK: True. It's not like that. The second step is to introduce a sacred symbol that expresses one's basic intention of consenting to God's presence and action within us.

RA: Visual symbol, auditory symbol, thought?

TK: It can be a word. It can be noticing the breath. It can be a simple inward glance towards that deeper self that I spoke of earlier.

RA: But it's not an external thing, not like some music you put on, or some image you think will be helpful.

TK: Right. It's totally receptive. It is a chance just to be with God alone and to say, "Here I am, dear Lord, at your disposal. Please heal my faults when you see that I am willing to let go of them." If you use a word, it's a single syllable. We call it a sacred word. It can be a name for God, or it can be something that expresses your disposition or attraction, like "love," or "peace," or "thanks."

RA: Or it could be a mantra like "om" or "shalom"?

TK: Yes, it could be.

RA: You are not chanting it out loud; it's mental.

TK: Yes. It is totally interior. You don't say it in centering prayer as a mantra that is repeated deliberately. You only use it when you need it—that is to say, when the bombardment of thoughts gets too noisy and you think you can't put up with it much longer.

RA: Let me just interject a question here that someone sent in to ask you on this very point. They said: "In your guidelines for centering prayer, one chooses a sacred word and introduces it with eyes closed. And when one becomes distracted by thoughts, one returns to the sacred word. What does one do between introducing the sacred word and before becoming distracted by thoughts, if one is just a beginner? Specifically speaking, does one introduce the sacred word once, or can one keep thinking the sacred word over and over again in the beginning stage?"

TK: The crucial distinction is, are you *having* thoughts or are you *engaged* in thoughts? If you are *having* thoughts, this is normal and impossible to avoid. The brain is a kind of receptor set and you can't do anything about that. The experience might be compared to a river with boats moving on top of it. You can't stop the boats, but you can stop yourself from getting on a boat to see what's in the hold. So you just let the thoughts come and let them go. As time goes on, the capacity to let go of thoughts promptly and easily becomes more and more second nature. But it takes time. It's not a onetime success story. You have to do it regularly because we have habits of constantly thinking about every blasted thing that happens. Centering prayer is an exercise in not thinking or detachment from thoughts when you can't stop thinking.

It's not that thinking is wrong. It's that we've abused it to the point where we can't think as a rule under our own initiative except when we have some special project we want to think about. You may notice you're engaged with a thought like, "What are we going to have for dinner?" As soon as you get into the contents of the meal, you're engaged. Then ever so gently you return to your sacred word as a symbol of your basic intention. This practice is not a success story. It's surrendering to the invitation of God to learn how to be. This is even more important than doing. You keep returning patiently to the sacred word again and again, maybe a hundred times in a single period of centering prayer.

You don't say it like you're hanging on to a life-preserver, because that would turn it into an egoic project. You don't look for success and you don't look for consolation. You are just present to God's presence and action, and renew that intention over and over again. You don't think about the sacred word or whatever your symbol is. You just *do* it. Sometimes, as you get more proficient, *to start to do it is enough*. In due time you experience an attraction towards a deeper silence. This is a sign that you've connected with this practice.

In that silence, which is consciousness without content, *presence* best describes it rather than thought or desire. It's a sense of being in God or God in you, or both, and wanting to be there. You continue the practice for about twenty minutes because it takes most people that much time to quiet down. We urge doing it twice a day. To quiet the mind requires a certain length of time and a regular practice because it is so co-opted by habits of thinking and choosing that are related to the three basic instincts of security, power and control, and affection and esteem.

RA: The body takes a while to settle down, too.

TK: Yes. As your defenses go down, purification begins. That is to say, thoughts that are in the unconscious that we repressed because they were too traumatic to handle in childhood begin to come to our awareness. We need to acknowledge them and give them to God. If you want to think about certain insights more fully, do so after the prayer is over.

RA: Will people be able to practice centering prayer based on our conversation, or is there some kind of formal instruction needed?

TK: We have formal instruction that we recommend, but some have picked up the practice from the books that describe it. The practice has a certain subtlety. It is as simple as could be. But simplicity for humans is the organization of much multiplicity. You may need the help of others as well as further training. We need to find a place for it in the very active lives that we lead in the American culture. This requires motivation and determination. We also urge people to realize how illusory the false self is. Sometimes the best preparation for centering prayer is some incident that brings to our attention just how little we actually know about God and the spiritual journey. It might be the time to find out!

RA: So if I were practicing centering prayer, and my sacred word was love, and I'm sitting there, I sit and close my eyes; maybe I wait for half a minute to let myself down a little bit.

TK: Good idea. A few deep breaths might help.

RA: A few deep breaths, and then I introduce the word "love," but I don't say "love, love, love." I just think it once. (I'm just repeating your instructions here.) Then I sit and enjoy the presence. The next thing, I notice I'm thinking about what I'm going to do tomorrow. As soon as I realize that I've wandered off on that thought, I just come back and think "love" again. That's pretty much the process, right?

TK: Right. When your twenty minutes is up, sit for another minute and a half or so to allow whatever has happened to settle down and work its way into your active faculties. This may bring a little of the peace you received during the prayer period into daily life and into relationships that are difficult.

RA: You were saying that as you settle into this deeply restful state, the repressed material buried in the nervous system and psyche begins to bubble up. Silence gives us the opportunity to release the emotional junk of a lifetime, which we can't do if we are running around like crazy people. Once we habitually settle down, we have the opportunity to start the spiritual journey of purification and inner freedom.

TK: Yes. The body naturally gets rid of negative or harmful influences if we allow it.

RA: It has a natural tendency to want to do that, right?

TK: Yes, but we are habituated not to do it or even not to know that it's possible to do anything different from what we have always done. We're pretty much enslaved to our cultural conditioning and habits of thought. We are always thinking about how to resolve problems instead of accepting them and moving on. Once we start accepting them, the sense of God's presence is likely to appear in daily life and events. And we become more sensitive to the divine action.

As I said, distracting thoughts are like boats moving down a river. The current will take them away if you just wait a minute. Just don't get on the boats; let them go by. That's the purpose of the sacred word. The practice of returning to the sacred word is not magical, nor has it any power of itself. It just gives the true self a chance to have a little breathing space.

In your relationships with others, you will often notice your faults, and you may reflect, "Why did I get so angry at that statement? My anger didn't seem proportionate." The Holy Spirit begins to show us how to improve our response to people, difficulties, and challenges.

Centering prayer helps us get through great trials, like suffering an immense loss. The prayer will help them let their feelings come and to grieve, and to let them go without being blown away as they used to be by difficulties or tragedy. This is something we all need in our time, when the media provide us with endless woes from all over the world. Every day, you get bombarded with violence and injustice everywhere in the world. This can't be good for people. We need some kind of a break. We have to figure out a way to balance the bad with the good, so we are not overwhelmed by depressing thoughts. We need to have some beauty to live in this world. Nature seems to be intended for that purpose.

RA: When people are sitting in centering prayer, and they enter a deeply restful state and some of this kind of repressed negativity or conflict begins to bubble up, can they expect to experience negative emotions, anger, fear, sadness?

TK: That's exactly what they experience.

RA: Turbulence?

TK: Whatever they repressed.

RA: It's got to come out.

TK: It needs to come out in order for the full capacities of the positive energies to function. These are the faculties of grace like love, compassion, forgiveness, understanding, the inclination to serve others, and knowing how to listen. All of these capacities buried under the load of our neglect or whatever upset us begin to thrive. I don't say negative thoughts and afflictive emotions are suddenly all taken away. But they won't blow you away the way they used to. If you keep doing this practice, you will be attracted to practices for daily life and also perhaps lengthen the time that you give to just sitting, waiting, listening, receptivity, and alert passivity. All these things are not very congenial to contemporary lifestyles. So they have to be learned. But the body and the human organism are completely prepared for this kind of holistic health and will revive, and you'll discover that you have the capacity for the unfolding of the contemplative journey within you. You don't have to try hard to do it, because it is basically a gift. Let it happen.

RA: It does you. You mention in your books that centering prayer is a preparation for contemplation, if I got you right. So it sounds like contemplation is a second stage of something.

TK: It depends on how you define "contemplation." If you mean the whole process of transformation, then centering prayer is the first step in the process. The fruits and gifts of the Spirit in prayer give one a sense of reassurance, of being loved by God, and that everything is OK. These contemplative dispositions don't arise all at once. But as you do the prayer, they begin to become more frequent—not only in prayer but in daily life.

RA: I see what you mean. It's as though centering prayer opens us up to a realm of experience that provides a foundation of sorts, and that almost spontaneously from that springs a greater sense of God's presence, of trust, of acceptance, of the inherent wisdom in the universe.

TK: And a perception of God's action in our daily lives. God brings people into our lives—sometimes through a book, phone call, or an event—to see something about ourselves that had been hidden from us or that will help our spiritual growth. In other words, we begin to enter into this psychotherapeutic relationship with God in which he deals with our psychological unconscious, temperamental defects, and personality disorders in a way that is almost incredible. The divine wisdom knows us through and through and still loves us infinitely. We see that God is gradually teaching us with the greatest patience, tenderness, and consideration. He waits for us and chooses just the right moment to give us a special grace, like on a retreat or some event in our lives that opens us to deep places in our emotional life.

There's nothing wrong with the emotions. It's mostly resisting them that is the problem, because we're often afraid of our feelings. Once we accept the fact that we are in God's care and in a therapeutic relationship with God, the inner room of contemplative prayer begins to expand to the whole of our life and everything we do. We can turn to God and say, "What shall I do about this? What do you want me to do?" In other words, there's a sense of companionship or even of being lived in.

As I say, sometimes God plays his games or he goes away without telling you, just to see what you will do with that, or whether you'll blame him, and how far you're willing to go in playing the divine games. One game he likes to play is basketball, with us as the ball. The harder the ball hits the floor, the higher it rises. So we have to learn that the bigger the trial, the greater the transformation that will come from it. We learn the way God works, which is not according to appearances. Another example: when you want to throw a basket, you have to dribble down the court. So the ball hits the floor: boom, boom, boom! That's when difficulties pile up, one right after another. But it's the only way you can reach the basket, if that's what you want to do.

RA: To recapitulate: You're saying that centering prayer, twenty minutes or so, twice a day, is not only restful in and of itself. But it will, over time, help to develop a kind of vision or view of the world that everything is divinely orchestrated; it's not arbitrary and capricious. There's actually a sort of loving intelligence, which we could call God, which is helping to bring about our progress and continuing evolution.

TK: Yes. In other words, you're in a relationship with God. This is the word many theologians today prefer to "person," because "person" has a certain context in the East. I found that many Eastern teachers thought that when we Christians spoke of God as a person, we were projecting on him a "personality," which of course would be a childish idea. God is not a person in that sense, but whatever he can be, he is. At least, he treats us in a personal way because that is the nature of our consciousness.

RA: Some Eastern perspectives have it that God has both impersonal and personal aspects.

TK: I would agree with that. He's impersonal with stones and he is personal with people. God is so accommodating. That is why the universe works in spite of all the astronomical catastrophes. Out of that immense chaos ultimately emerges human consciousness, which is the greatest masterpiece of creation. That is still going on. If we could collaborate with it, we have no idea what wonderful things the human race might be capable of in the next millennium.

RA: If we think of what the human race may be capable of, perhaps we could get a hint by seeing what an individual is capable of, if that individual really progresses far along on the spiritual path. Maybe at this phase of the interview, you could lay out for us what you see as a kind of road map of spiritual progress from very preliminary stages to the ultimate stage, if there is an ultimate stage. What does a person go through? What have you gone through over these decades?

TK: It's not anything I expected for sure. I've been a poor playmate for the wonderful opportunities that God has given me. But I think that if you put human development in the context of evolution, you see that there is a certain unity of purpose, organization, and experience. Like in biology, the earlier forms of life grow by increasing movement and complexity. Then, when humans arise, new levels of consciousness appear.

As humans, we don't know how we started out. That's a matter of controversy among the religions. All that we know as of now is that the human development theories of Jean Piaget (1896–1980) recapitulates the whole movement of evolutionary progress from matter to life, more complex and conscious forms of life capable of more and more refined movement, and finally to higher forms of life.

Our spiritual journey and our relationship with God reflect that context. We start off as children thinking of God as "Dad" and "Mom," like the father and mother who are parenting us. Later on, God becomes a companion, friend, or soul mate; and then he becomes a lover, a person we are engaged to, or our spouse. We can also look upon God as fulfilling all kinds of other relationships. In other words, God is so adaptable you can count on him for any relationship. But there's a certain progression of intimacy and transformation that takes place in human development that involves a communion with God that is permanent and signals the possibility of further consciousness.

The spiritual journey seems to be integrating our turbulent daily life of floundering. Things have to be done to survive in this world and yet at the same time we're called to the most sublime communion that can be conceived of and to become, as far as possible for a creature, equal to God. Why he chose this plan, you'll have to ask him! But it seems to be occurring in outstanding mystics, contemplatives, sages, and saints. Catholics celebrate in the liturgy of the feast of Epiphany the grace of bridal union with God and with Christ.

What happens after that? Transforming union introduces one to a whole new set of circumstances, capabilities, and possibilities, which move towards what is called "non-dual consciousness," "unity consciousness," or the "death of the separate-self sense." The sense of a separate self is the ultimate cause of all our problems in the first place, even more fundamental than the false self. The developing infant looks for happiness in the gratification of its desires for unlimited security, affection, and independence. This can only lead to various degrees of frustration.

The goal is to move into the realization that our deepest self is God's presence in us, which does not forestall our uniqueness but which manifests the divine dispositions in this creature who hasn't yet evolved from animal consciousness to be fully human. We still have the animal brain that we have to have to survive in this life. The divine and the human in the evolutionary process are battling to see whether we're going to evolve into divine-human beings, or whether we're going to keep regressing to the instinctual responses of our animal nature, which lead to violence and all the other negative emotions that hinder us from moving individually and a society into divine union.

RA: I know you're a modest man and you may not want to talk about your own experience, but have you gone through the stages that you just described in that union with God and then further maturation into non-dual unity?

TK: I'm working on it. It's not a ski tow that takes you non-stop to the top of a slope. It's something I'm working on all the time. Having lived to be ninety, I can see there's a lot of work yet on my unconscious that God could do in order that all my actions may be moved by Christ living within me. Christ become one of us in order to make us into what he is, sharers in the divine life.

Jesus said, "The Father and I are one." This is not a numerical assertion, but an equality of life and consciousness in which everything is saturated with the divine presence and that might be identified, as it is in scripture, as the "house of God," or the bosom of God. If you prefer a fleshy image, it could be imagined as the womb of God. In any case, we all must go through the dying process as the birth canal to eternal life.

RA: When you consider the size of the universe, it's vast, beyond comprehension. These days, they're finding planets around most stars and a good many of them apparently in what they call the Goldilocks zone, which can be habitable, not too hot and not too cold. Let's presume that the universe is actually teeming with life and that a good deal of that life has evolved to at least the level of our species. How does Christ fit in with all that? We think of Christ as this guy who lived two thousand years ago. Would he be on tour, going to all these inhabited places? Or does each planet have its own Christ, and is Christ more of a universal principle that was manifested in Jesus of Nazareth, but that could also be manifest in billions of other highly evolved souls who are ministering to their respective planets?

TK: We don't know the answers to those questions. But we don't have to be afraid of them if we have a Christian perspective, because the Word made flesh in Jesus is also made flesh in each of us. We are incarnations of God too, but in a much more limited sense. Christ is believed to be a divine person possessing a human nature. We are going to participate in a similar relationship with God as we negotiate our complex journey into non-duality and liberation from the false self and ego. The false self and ego have no future. They are illusions, and so God can't support them. But we do need a developed ego to survive in this world. How you deal with that is precisely the conundrum or the paradox of everyday life.

RA: Don't you find that there is something multi-dimensional in your own experience, where you have an ego, which you need functionally in order to get through the door and go and eat lunch? On the other hand, you know there are dimensions that are beyond the ego, that are impersonal, and somehow all those strata coexist nicely together.

TK: That's what is called "simplicity," which takes place when all the levels of which human nature are composed is integrated one with the other in a hierarchical fashion. That doesn't mean that one's state of life is necessarily better than another, but it does mean that we are different; and that the difference is important to the overall completion of what the Christians call "the mystical body of Christ."

Christ was at work from the beginning of time. The man Jesus Christ is a historical figure, Christians believe, possessed by the Word of God, which is not the same as Christ as God. Christ as God can continue to have manifestations of the Word of God on other planets. But it's basically the same movement that is expressed in different ways. It would not be the historical context that we are familiar with on planet earth.

It's going to take a lot of ingenuity to figure out how to get to these other planets. They are a long way off. Scientists may figure out a way of going faster than light, but it may take a long time. However, we need to be prepared to deal someday with a new kind of intelligence in bodily form. If these people are better than us, how are we going to get on? We have to grow out of the narrow mindedness of the human race that puts nation or religion ahead of the basic goodness of being human.

RA: If we do go there, I think what we'll find is that very same presence of God is just as much saturating everything there as it is right here.

TK: Absolutely.

RA: In that sense, we're already there.

TK: Teilhard de Chardin says that God is present in every subatomic particle. That is another way of saying God is omnipresent or everywhere.

RA: That's sort of how we started this discussion.

TK: There's another factor we may discover, which is that time and space may be just constructions of our intellect, and of our way of seeing the world. There may be planets that have a different kind of structure. God will be just as present there but in a different way. Perhaps if you think of yourself as an icon of God or a unique expression of the

Word made flesh, God's initial response to Job comes into a new focus.

If you can recall that story, Job got very angry with God because he felt mistreated. He had been a very highly respected man, but God, according to the text, allowed him to be tempted by the devil. Job was battered by every kind of human tragedy: loss of family, reputation, business, illness (he finally found his entire body covered with sores). His friends came to console him and plied him with pious platitudes. His response was, "I didn't do anything wrong. God is unjust and I want to bring him to judgment." God finally appears and just his presence answers all Job's questions. God then restores him to ten times as many blessings as he had before.

God opens his conversation with Job by saying, "Where were you when I formed the cosmos, made the stars, and fixed the earth?" (Job 38:4) Was God ironically teasing him, or was God actually trying to lead him to a new understanding of who Job actually was? God may have been trying to evoke from Job the answer: "I was there, too!" As if to say, "You were always co-creating with me, and we will be creating everything together in the future." In other words, equality with God is quite an invitation! Why do people want to become big shots in this world when we have all received a gilt-edged invitation to become one with God? In other words, we don't think *big* enough about God! We judge him by our own limitations and negative feelings, and then project those feelings onto him.

RA: Sometimes God wants to play at being president of a company. If someone could be president of a company, and yet aware of their oneness with God, we might have better companies.

TK: We will have to do a little more evolving to get to that place, but it's certainly within the range of possibilities. If people would put their minds on becoming God—not in the sense of power, but in the sense of serving every living thing as far as they have the strength and talents to do so— then the world would become the Garden of Eden. In fact, we have to make it the Garden of Eden or we will make it into a kind of hell. The false self has the tendency to create its own hell and which can start in this life.

RA: Some Christians would hear you say that and consider it blasphemous, but it bears repeating that you're not talking about the individual false self becoming God. You're talking about realization of that level of life at which we and God are one.

TK: Yes, and discovering that it has always been that way from the beginning. We just thought it was different because we didn't have the experience that could teach us.

Centering prayer is a very humble start consisting of just sitting down, shutting up, and letting God be God.

RA: That's a useful tool.

TK: The bottom line is always love, and loving God with our whole mind, heart, soul, and strength. That's the vision statement of the Judeo-Christian religions. To love one another as God has loved us, or at least as we love ourselves, is our mission. Centering prayer is designed to further that project.

RA: I've really enjoyed this discussion because, although I have never been a religious person, I, over the years, have gotten more and more appreciative of God, and sometimes discussions in contemporary spirituality are somewhat dry. They emphasize the absolute value without any kind of divine quality to it. And that doesn't jive with my orientation or my experience. So it's been delightful reading your books and having this conversation with someone for whom that orientation has been very strong for your entire life.

TK: I still have lots to do. If he has called us, as the bible says he has, there's nothing to be afraid of. Whatever we are scared of we need to sit with it and give to God. Gratitude, trust in God, and self-surrender: those are the transformations of consciousness we are working towards in contemplative prayer.

Religion needs to make sure that it is leading and teaching people to go in this direction. Otherwise, it's not really meeting its purpose and getting too involved in externals, rituals, or structures. They are important, but only up to a point; they are not ends in themselves. God can work independently of religion. He has many ways of bringing people to himself. Some people have been so damaged by religious misinformation or malformation that they can no longer go by that path. God is sheer freedom, liberation, and this total freedom is the disposition that we are being invited into, so that we can be God, too, without pride or attributing anything to ourselves.

RA: It occurred to me as you said that, that everything has something to contribute. Religion has something to contribute; science has something to contribute. The non-religious sort of spirituality that's in vogue these days—people say, "I'm spiritual but not religious"—has something to contribute. If all these people could just let their guard down a little bit and be open to the gifts that each has to give, then there would be a mutual enrichment that would make everything more vibrant and healthy.

TK: You're describing the goal of the interspiritual movement.

RA: Well, my take on it is that we have reason for optimism. The signs are there as you were saying earlier on. There is a kind of mass awakening taking place, and somehow all these intractable problems and institutions that seem to be so opposed to human happiness and betterment don't stand a chance. Everything will either fall away or transform itself as this invincible upwelling of Spirit takes place, as it seems to be doing with greater and greater force and speed.

TK: It's amazing how God makes use of very defective instruments to bring about amazing results. But we may have to wait. To be united to God is what gives God most glory. He will turn the world upside down to bring someone who is willing to unity-consciousness.

Thank you for your interest in the transformative process. It is the most important issue for human beings.

PART II

REFLECTIONS
ON THE
UNKNOWABLE

1

THE BLACK VESTMENT

A T St. Joseph's monastery in Valley Falls, Rhode Island, where I lived before the fire of March 21, 1950, destroyed virtually the entire complex, there was a black vestment in the sacristy with a purple velvet band in the back that was used regularly for requiem masses. That single strand of velvet parted in the back and continued over each shoulder. At the center of the band was an image of the head and neck of an eagle, its beak pointing straight up and emphasizing one of its eyes, an eye filled with anguish and longing.

The eagle's eye depicted for me the longing for union with God of a soul in purgatory or in the night of spirit, which the Spanish mystic Saint John of the Cross (1542–1591) calls the equivalent of purgatory. The bird's gaze seemed to express the unfulfilled desire of such a soul to be completely united to God, and if that were not possible, the wish to cease to exist. The gaze seemed to articulate an all-consuming longing uniting all the powers of the human person—body, soul, and spirit—into a movement of total self-surrender to God. One's whole life and being in that state is centered in an interior gaze of longing love that wants only God. It wants to be purified of every obstacle in itself. It knows its capacity for evil and wants "to know nothing among you except Jesus Christ, and him Crucified" (1 Corinthians 2:2).

The eagle's eye symbolized for me the anguished look of one with an unbearable desire for pure love: to lose itself in the tender and all-consuming mercy of God. The lack of divine union and its limitless joy brings enormous pain, privation, and sense of loss: suffering that is immeasurable, indescribable, and inconceivable, but nonetheless very real. No relief, healing, or peace can be found anywhere until this monumental confrontation of opposites—the being of God and the being of a human person—is resolved. Waiting for God, living with the feeling of powerlessness, is perhaps the most direct path to the resolution of these opposites and to inner peace.

To be powerless is *to accept and welcome all the consequences of being powerless*. It is to feel oneself to be weakness itself, unable to practice even the smallest virtue, and to be always failing in one's good intentions and resolutions. It is to die at every moment into utter spiritual destitution. It is to be nailed to the cross in union with Christ. It is to live in Christ and to let Christ live in us. Saint Paul puts it succinctly: "It is no longer I who live, but it is Christ who lives in me" (Galatians 2:20).

2

THE SCIENCE OF LOVE

A GLOBAL CHRISTIANITY MUST BE based on the practice of servant leadership, rooted in an established contemplative practice and adapted by each denomination to its own particular circumstances and theological traditions. It must be open to partnerships with the spiritual disciplines and traditions of other religions and include in the dialogue scientists and people of no religion. Contemplation when fully developed is the highest realization of the unity of science and religion. It is *the science of love*.

In the Christian religion, the Holy Trinity is the central and deepest mystery of its faith. The Father is emptiness containing infinite possibilities. The Son is all that is possible in the Father's emptiness coming to actuality. The Spirit is the love that rushes back and forth between the Father and the Son, never satisfied with just one and

not the other. Divine love attracts all to itself. It is irresistible. We have to run after it no matter how many times we
stumble. According to Thomas Aquinas (1225–1274), we
were created with a boundless capacity to receive it.

These three relationships are one reality, or rather what
is beyond all reality including Reality itself.

Jesus Christ in his teaching seems less interested in raising
us to enlightened states of consciousness than in becoming
one with us in the events and experiences of ordinary daily
life. To relive the sacred mysteries of his earthly life in each
of us is his plan and desire; to share every moment of our
lives with him is the practical living out of divine union. His
presence in us is our deepest self manifesting in every action,
however trivial from our point of view. We are invited to
have no movement of body, mind, and heart except from the
Spirit, who wishes to inspire all our thoughts, words, and
actions.

If we are bored in meditation, unequal to a task, weak
in facing temptation, distracted in prayer, or tormented
by afflicting emotions; if we feel powerless to practice any
virtue, abandoned by God, experience inward ground-
lessness, and suffer endless guilt—it is Jesus in us and *as*
us who is suffering everything. He is living our lives all
the time if we consent to be who we really are. Wisdom
entails dropping all efforts to fix anything including ourselves. The Spirit will do the changing. Efforts to make our
self acceptable to God will not succeed.

Christ is returning to the Father in us. He empties himself, giving back to the Father all he has received. In the degree that we let go of the separate-self sense, we enter into the movement of his return to the Father and are drawn by the irresistible attraction of divine love. We long to become one with that love, to be immersed in its infinite flow within the Trinity, fulfilling Jesus' petition to the Father in his final discourse at the Last Supper, "that they may all be one even as we are one" (John 17:21).

Christ is returning to the Father in every circumstance, however horrendous, inhuman, or sinful. To want to return to periods of felt union with God and spiritual consolation is natural to us, but is usually based on an egoic attachment to some spiritual experience that was delightful in the past.

To hope for something better in the future is not the theological virtue of hope. Theological hope is based on God alone, who is both infinitely merciful and infinitely powerful *right now.*

Here is a formula to deepen and further the theological virtue of hope with its unbounded confidence in God. Let whatever is happening happen and go on happening. Welcome whatever it is. Let go into the present moment by surrendering to its content. We may cry for help, but it is not necessary. God is always eager to heal needless suffering and to sustain our weakness.

The divine energies are rushing past us at every nanosecond of time. Why not reach out and catch them by continuing acts of self-surrender and trust in God? The proper response to God's abundance is to consent to his presence and surrender to his action within us.

Let Christ live within you as you. This is resurrection—what Jesus calls (in his words to Martha) "the resurrection and the life" (John 11:25).

At least one school of Zen Buddhism teaches, "Everything just as it is, is perfect." That means, I presume, that possibilities for human growth are part of every reality including suffering.

Inner freedom is the source of the greatest creativity. God is gradually entrusting the future of the species to us, while remaining our partner and companion. In this way, God makes us (in a real sense) equal to himself: co-creators and co-redeemers.

Jesus "spat on the ground and made mud with the saliva and spread the mud on the man's eyes" (John 9:6). This scene is a symbol of the interpenetration of the divine with the human; in other words, the incarnation of Christ in us which the union of the ultimate opposites, the divine and the human. It is the divine kiss—mouth to mouth, heart to heart, being to being—the pouring of the divine light, life, and love into our limitless capacity for God. It is the gift of the Spirit, the ripe fruit of Christ's resurrection. This is his gift to the apostles on the night of his resurrection. "Receive the Holy Spirit" (John 20:22) is the divine breath that contains the whole of God and all that exists.

There is no effort needed to receive the divine breath. Breathing is inherent to human nature on both the physical and spiritual levels. It constantly happens. Our best effort is no effort: just to receive intentionally—that is, with total consent—the continuous divine communication.

The will is the mouth of the soul. The Spirit is the divine breath. Letting go of every form of self-identity or reflection is the nature of pure consciousness: to surrender to God just as we are and to surrender to God just as God is.

The Father is infinite possibilities, the great nothingness—indeed absolute Nothingness. The Son is all that the Father is—every possibility fully realized, fully actualized. The Spirit is the love of everything according to its nature. The capacity for intimacy with God is in proportion to our consent to be a creature and our willingness to remain so. The acceptance of powerlessness is the path to becoming everything and to be truly like God, equal to God in every way that is possible for a creature.

It is not pride or ambition to want to love God as he has never yet been loved. But others more advanced along the continuing evolutionary spiral may love him still more, or in new ways. Yet, what does "more" really mean when each human being is unique and thus a unique manifestation of God?

To surrender to God just as God is, is to accept his all-inclusive intelligence manifested by the divine plan of creation, redemption, and transformation through the evolutionary process. It is to appreciate the wisdom of his care for each creature according to its nature, need, and capacity. It is to be in awe and boundlessly grateful for his patience, forgiveness, guidance, consolation, the amazing intimacy of his presence, and his continuous sharing of the divine life and love.

Consider the pain of the Father in losing his beloved Son and the pain of the Son in causing the Father to reject him, which identifying with the sins of the world inevitably involved.

The Father, on his part, knew that his Son would be rejecting him by being "made sin," but such was his will. He chose the anguish of loss and separation out of a greater love. Since the Father lives in the Son rather than in himself, he died with the Son in the latter's death upon the cross.

What died? Was it their relationship of infinite love, at least for that moment? The death of Jesus manifested the eternal emptying of the Father, the ultimate surrender of infinite life and all the divine attributes: a movement of a love beyond love, a reality that cannot be conceived but only worshipped.

The death of Jesus also expressed the full extent of the love of the Father for human beings and their desperate need for security, love, and freedom. This love sought to make them participators in the Trinitarian relationships, equal in every possible way to God. *Deification* as the purpose of creation and not just to become good persons. For the Eastern churches, *deification* is the term that we use in the West for *transformation in Christ*.

Only the Son in his suffering, death, and descent into hell—three stages of identification with sin—could make the depths of the Father's humility and love completely manifest in human consciousness.

God made himself equal to us in the incarnation by identifying with the human condition. Grace makes us equal to God through the forgiveness of every sin and by transforming us into his own unconditional love.

Sin and addictive behavior reduce consciousness to a narrow, blind, and compulsive focus of attention directed to self-centered gratifications. Perception becomes very limited and attention is battered by a barrage of images, reflections, and scenarios that impose themselves on our consciousness, suspending due regard for the consequences of acting out instinctive needs and impulses.

Christ's forgiveness transforms the wounds that deliberate sins inflict upon him into what the Spanish mystic Saint Teresa of Avila (1515–1582) called "fountains of pure love." It is not just restoration or return to original innocence (before self-consciousness arose), but something brand new: a share in the divine innocence and the transformation of the wounds of sin into divine love and interior freedom.

God's gift of freedom from all sin and every inclination towards it is the freedom to love.

3

ARE THERE PERSONS
IN THE TRINITY?

"PERSON" IS AN AMBIGUOUS term in our time when psychology and theology are beginning to speak in depth to each other. In early Christian theology, "person" was a term used by the Council of Nicaea (325) in its discussion of the two natures in Christ, as understood by the majority of the church fathers at that Council. According to the teaching of the incarnation accepted by the Council, Jesus is not a human person, but a human being *possessed* by the person of the Word, the Son of God, whom Saint Paul designates as Christ. According to the Council, there are two natures in Christ, one fully human and the other fully divine, united without any confusion of the two. In this view, Christ is the one to whom all the actions of the man Jesus of Nazareth are to be attributed.

The classical definition of "person" in Christian theology is "a unique substance possessing intelligence and will." In this view, a purely spiritual being would also be a person, though it would lack a personality since the latter requires the functioning of the life of the external senses. In this sense, we might say that Christ (the Eternal Word of God) is not only a person, but *every* person.

If Christ, as the Eternal Word of God, possesses the human nature of Jesus (the Word made flesh), he must relate to us in a personal way.

In his divine nature, the Absolute also relates to us in an impersonal way, as experienced in Buddhism. The basic experience of Buddhism and Christianity is ultimately reconcilable.

Some contemporary theologians are of the mind that "person" is not the best term to designate the distinctions in the Trinity and prefer the term "relationship." How the three relationships of the holy Trinity relate to each other is precisely the mystery of the Trinity itself, which acts in creation as one.

4

SPIRITUAL EVOLUTION

SPIRITUAL EVOLUTION IS A process of liberation. It completes biological evolution, which has brought us to the relative freedom of rational consciousness. But full access to that stage of development is limited by attachment to lower forms of consciousness that are not free. Beyond rational consciousness, the path to interior freedom expands to become a union of wills with that which is Freedom itself.

Spiritual evolution is the path of liberation from the false self, the ego, and the separate-self sense. These illusions are the source of human misery, limitation, and sin. The process of spiritual evolution opens not only to the union of wills between God and us in the abiding state of transforming union, but to participating in the very freedom of Ultimate Reality.

The spiritual traditions of the various religions are normally designed to be paths to the experience of Ultimate Reality. Why not be open to them all, and thus to complement the practical wisdom provided by one's own spiritual tradition?

"No one can come to me unless drawn by the Father who sent me" (John 6:44). How does the Father draw us? God cannot exercise the full ardor of his will to force us to become one with him without compromising the relative freedom that he has given us. Inner freedom is the very essence of the image and likeness of God in which, according to the book of Genesis, we were created.

God initially hides behind words that sometimes sound commanding, limiting, and even threatening. By these admonitions he awakens a sense of responsibility for our behavior and then accountability for our actions. He draws us along the path of liberation from the false self, our emotional programs for happiness, our over-identification with and excessive dependency on the various groups to which we belong, and from the separate-self sense—that is, from attachment to any self at all. What remains when this process is completed is the divine Self manifesting in us. For Christians, this is the grace of the Ascension. In and with Christ's Ascension, we enter into the bosom of the Father and lose ourselves in the love that rushes with boundless delight between the Trinitarian relationships.

"I and the Father are one" (John 10:30). This statement

affirms the distinction and yet the perfect unity of the Trinitarian relationships. Jesus prayed to the Father at the Last Supper, "That they may be one, as we are one, I in them and you in me, that they may become completely one, so that the world may know that you have sent me and have loved them even as you have loved me" (John 17:22–23).

The highest call of humanity is to manifest the Un-manifested, or more precisely, *the Un-manifestable*. Ultimately, there is only THAT WHICH IS. Rational consciousness is a major step along the evolutionary way, but it is only the beginning. We must bring our conscious presence to the divine presence and all that we are—body, soul, and spirit—to all that God is in order to receive all that God is.

5

KENOSIS

*K*ENOSIS IS ANOTHER WORD for God's humility, which is infinite. God is not a thing, not an object. God is the subjectivity in which all things great or small reside. God is One. All that exists is in him. Or better, God is always *One-ing* with all that exists.

God is also the inconceivable, the *mysterium tremendum*—that which there is no other. In this perspective God is "all in all" (1 Corinthians 15:28).

The Son's self-emptying (*kenosis*) reaches its peak in the incarnation, where Jesus in his passion, death, and descent into hell is "made sin," the very opposite of God. In the jungle of human freedom where pride reigns, the humanity of Jesus becomes identified with the consequences of sin: the sense of alienation, loneliness, isolation.

To be a follower of Christ is to identify with Jesus *as*

sin, including the psychological and sociological consequences. It is to join the crucified in his descent into hell, the psychological state of alienation from God, others, and one's true self.

To be a follower is to let Christ, the eternal Son of God, express in our human nature God's inclination *not* to be God and to know what hell is by personal experience; but at the same time to endure this state with invincible hope in the Father's boundless compassion and forgiveness.

Divine love has to give itself away in the most absolute manner in order to bear witness to the fact that the humility of God has no limits. Humility has to take the lowest place.

To love, welcome, and to go on choosing to remain powerless, while hoping to be audacious about the Father's goodness is the essential disposition of the path of kenosis—the disposition that the French mystic Saint Thérèse of Lisieux (1873–1897) described as "being a victim of divine love."

The Eternal Word of God emerges from the silence of the Father. Everything created emerges from the silence of the Word and returns to the Father together with the incarnate Word. Through the practice of interior silence, forgetfulness of self, and the humble service of others, the Son returns to the Father in us, and we return to the Father in him.

6

CHRIST THE CENTER
OF THE SOUL

GOD IS PRESENT IN everything, but not limited by anything.

Being is relationship with everything that exists, and everything that exists is in relationship with God.

According to Saint John of the Cross, "the inmost center of the soul is Christ." Through the incarnation, God identified with humankind, the lowest of intelligent creatures that we know of in the cosmos. This identification may be what turned the angels against God. Seeing their Beloved becoming the very opposite of God in the passion and death of Jesus may have given them more grief than they could handle. They may have experienced the humiliation of Jesus as a rejection of *them*. Some of the powers of the angelic world may have refused to consent to the experience of what they perceived as the loss of their angelic superiority.

The Father is always begetting the Son. All the possibilities hidden in the Father are actualizing in the Son. Through the Spirit, the Son returns to the Father, to the silence that belongs to the One who manifests all that he is in the Son. The Spirit is the outpouring of the love of the Father and the Son in the Trinity and throughout all creation.

To become a *thou*, someone has to address us and tell us that we are loved. Through the great I AM addressing us in the experience of being loved, we come to life in God.

The false self and our willfulness create our own personal hells. God offers us heaven. When there is no more sense of an "I" (ego), the great I AM takes over our lives.

In Christ, the divine hits bottom: he "emptied himself" (Philippians 2:7). There is no place for him to go but up; from this perspective death is the birth canal to eternal life.

The passion of Jesus is the evacuation of sin and its consequences (egoic activity) from the collective body of the universe: in Christian terms, *from the mystical body of Christ.* To extend this process throughout space and time, certain cells in the mystical body are called to collaborate in building up the health of this body and healing the cells that are diseased. The proclamation of the liturgy, "Lamb of God, You take away the sin of the world" is a way of expressing this reality. Some are called to be the evacuation channels of the universe through whom the mystical body is constantly liberated from the negative consequences of sin.

The Word of God, named Jesus (Savior) by divine command, was active before the incarnation. The Word and its activity are not limited by the historical reality of the man Jesus, whose humanity it possessed. The Eternal Word may have manifested in other persons, such as Krishna, Laozi, Buddha, Muhammad, and in the teaching of the Absolute in Buddhism, the Upanishads, Advaita Vedanta, and other experiences of the divine. These were channels of bringing divine love into the world.

According to the prologue of Saint John's Gospel, Jesus is the Word of God who became one with the human condition. The consequences of God's identification with the human condition are his lifelong redeeming activity.

If the human condition as we experience it (weakness, sin, alienation, loneliness, and at times hellishness) is not the fault of Adam and Eve, then it must in some way be God's responsibility.

Can we forgive God for placing us in such an impossible (at least to us) situation? According to Saint Paul, God was reconciling the world to himself in Christ (Colossians 1:20).

7

THE UNIQUENESS OF JESUS

THE ONE WHO IS (Ultimate Reality) is also Abba, the creator of all, the sustainer of all, the lover of all, the one who holds each of us and every creature in an everlasting and tender embrace.

The source of everyone's capacity to become divine is rooted in the Eternal Word of God becoming flesh and identifying with human nature and with each human being in his or her uniqueness. Jesus is unique among the spiritual giants who founded the world's religions or renewed them. He was not only a fully enlightened human being. After his death he was proclaimed by his disciples as the Son of God made human in every respect except sin. The human race in virtue of God becoming one of its members is one body with Christ Jesus as its head. He fills the whole human family backwards and forwards in time with his divine energy, dignity, and grace in a way not possible for a merely human teacher.

The purpose of Jesus' revelation of the Father is to awaken us to the image and likeness of God in which we were created (Genesis 1:26). This image, according to the story of Adam and Eve, was not lost by their fall. The likeness, however, was severed by the separate-self sense that awakened in them after they ate the fruit of the tree of good and evil, a symbol of the awakening of self-consciousness. After consuming that fruit, the couple fled into the woods to escape from their horrendous feelings of shame and guilt.

We come to self-consciousness without the prior experience of God's loving presence and action within us; hence we have no criteria or standard on which to base our idea of what true happiness really is or might be.

The call to return to the innocence of our first parents through the dying of the separate-self sense is the call to access the state of consciousness symbolized by the Garden of Eden, which represents intimacy with God. As presented in the Genesis story, it is the recovery of the likeness of God lost by the fall of our first parents from innocence into the experience of their false selves.

The false self manifests itself in the emotional programs for happiness built upon the instinctual needs of human nature for survival and security, affection and esteem, and power and control, as well as over-identification with the social groups to which we belong. The latter takes place during our socialization period from about four to eight years of age. The primary activity of the false self is the gratification of its instinctual needs and the acceptance by our social group. The true source of human happiness, which is the experience of God's living presence, is unknown to it.

In this perspective, the incarnation and Redemption (Jesus' passion, death, and resurrection) goes much further in manifesting God's infinite goodness and love for the human family than the healing of the consequences of the fall of Adam and Eve, incredible as such love actually is.

The work of our salvation and sanctification is manifested by the totality of the Son's gift of himself to us in his passion and death. *Transmission* might be a better word than *manifested*, since the gift is the divine reality itself.

The eternal Son from the beginning is by nature one with the Father. The Father is all possibilities coming to consciousness in the Son. The Son gives himself totally to the Father in the surrender of all that he receives. Through their mutual surrender, they live in each other rather than in themselves. From their total self-giving proceeds the Holy Spirit, the bond of their unity and the celebration of their boundless love. The Holy Spirit reconstitutes the Father and the Son in their relationship of unity with the Godhead and of infinite diversity in regard to each other. In that diversity we are called to become both fully human and fully divine.

8

ARE WE INCARNATIONS
OF CHRIST?

A LONG WITH THE SEPARATE-SELF sense arises
the false self and the gradual emergence of the ego.
All three manifest the characteristics identified in classical Christian theology as the consequences of original sin:
illusion (not knowing where to look for happiness), concu-
piscence (seeking it in limited and impossible places), and
weakness of will (the inability to pursue effectively the true
sources of happiness, even when we know where to look).

The root of all sin is the separate-self sense. The deliberate dismantling of the false self and the death of the ego
is the narrow gate "that leads to life" (Matthew 7:14): the
straight, direct, and shortest way to divine union, human
wholeness, and boundless happiness.

The separate-self sense, beginning even in the womb,
seems to be an inevitable accompaniment of human devel-

opment and growth. To what do we attribute the separate-self sense? The book of Genesis proposes that it is the result of the fall from grace of our first parents and that it affects their entire human progeny, depriving it of the divine intimacy symbolized by the Garden of Eden.

Contemporary science proposes that the separate-self sense is part of the evolutionary process from mammalian to human consciousness.

The Perennial Philosophy, represented in various forms in the world religions, affirms that there are further states of consciousness beyond the rational. The vast majority of the human species, however, has not yet evolved into them.

We become in some real sense incarnations of Christ in the sacrament of baptism when we are incorporated into his mystical body. But the full development of all the possibilities of baptism normally takes a lifetime.

According to the four Gospels, God sent his only begotten Son to heal (redeem) the human family. Just what does this healing consist of?

The account of the fall in Genesis tends to communicate a profound sense of guilt and of personal accountability for the fall even though, at least according to Roman Catholic theologies, there is no personal sin on our part.

Because we are members of one species, all of whom are interconnected and interdependent, our every thought, word, and deed affect everyone else in the human family instantaneously, regardless of space and time. Hence, we are accountable to each other as well as to God.

The present moment is always changing, always new. To respond, one must establish a certain spiritual poise like a cruising speed on a freeway. To think is to apply the brakes. It slows you down. You might even have to stop at the side of the road.

What maintains normal speed on the spiritual journey are not ideas but intuitions. Such are the inspirations of the fruits and gifts of the Spirit. In prayer, not thinking but *being* is the primary goal. Thinking *about* ourselves is not *it*.

"One Christ loving himself" is Saint Augustine's description of the mystical body of Christ. There are distinctions by way of service but no basic inequalities. All are one; we just have different functions in the body of Christ, as Saint Paul explains (cf. 1 Corinthians 12:4–31).

9

ONENESS

IN ONENESS, THERE IS not more or less; there is only oneness. I used the term *One-ing* earlier as a more accurate term because it is always happening. God is not an object or a noun as we understand those terms. God just *is, is, is.* One-ing is to be, to live, and to act. Christ is Saint Paul's name for the only begotten Son of God whom the Father is forever begetting. Jesus is the unique and complete incarnation of the Son of God; humans might be seen as partial incarnations.

The statement that Christ Jesus is the one "whom the Father has sanctified and sent into the world" (John 10:36) describes Jesus' vocation. He did not come of his own volition. He was sent by the Father to "proclaim the good news to the whole creation" (Mark 16:15).

That God's will may "be done, on earth as it is in heaven" (Matthew 6:10) is Jesus' personal prayer for the full development of human consciousness. Hence, he has taught us to ask and prepare for the actualization of this grace and for the awakening of contemplation, which is the normal means to experience it.

Divine wisdom in the book of Wisdom is represented as creating, sustaining, and expanding creation, manifesting in infinite diversity the oneness of the divine ground. Wisdom creates matter and all forms out of the silence (emptiness) of the ground. Matter, and the life into which it evolves, manifest the divine intelligence and Being beyond being. Wisdom, the Word of God manifesting the Father, is always coming into creation and always returning to the Father.

The glory of the risen Christ is returning to the Father in its most triumphant form—the humiliation of being the last, least, lowest, and most despised of creatures. The Trinitarian humility is boundless, exquisitely beautiful, compassionate, relentlessly overcoming all evil, transforming sin itself into pure love.

The human creature with the gift of free choice—the image of God in us—easily sees itself as a competitor of God "knowing good and evil." It wants to be God on its own terms, a project Satan suggested in tempting Adam and Eve to disobey the creator (Genesis 3:1–7).

To be the servant of God is to be willing to accept God's invitation to be God *on God's terms*. This amazing proposal may seem intolerable to human pride and a misuse of the extraordinary creativity we have received. Accordingly, we need to distinguish carefully the no-self that is God-made and the no-self that is self-made.

10

ARE WE GOD'S THOUGHTS?

Jesus' description of the Last Judgment reveals his loving concern for the needy: for those in prison, the sick and the dying, those deprived of education, the hungry and the homeless, bonded labor and those enslaved to the sex trade, the pornographic industry, and the whole vast range of the military-industrial complex. God created us in weakness and with freedom to accept or reject his love. He became a human being in order to experience first-hand what the human condition is like—immersing himself in it by becoming human in every respect except sin.

Knowing our weakness, God created us in Christ so that our sins could never be a hindrance to union with him. The natural sanctions of personal and collective sin, however, could not be entirely prevented and emerge as feelings of guilt and the physical and emotional damage inflicted on us by ourselves and others. Yet, all punishment was taken away by Christ or never existed in the first place.

The grace of the Holy Spirit contained in the mystical body of Jesus Christ is poured into our inmost being through his broken body, symbol of his identification with the human condition. The only requirement to receive it is our consent to the healing and redeeming activity of Jesus in virtue of our incorporation through faith in his mystical body.

The Eucharist is the bread of life: the divine food from heaven. Contemplative prayer is the nutritional process of consuming the bread of life: Christ in the Eucharist.

Spiritual nutrition consists of two processes: assimilation of nutrients—the fruits and gifts of the Spirit—and the evacuation of useless or harmful materials: purification.

The term *faith* normally means *trust* when it occurs in the bible, especially in the New Testament. It is not so much the acceptance of doctrinal and dogmatic proclamations as self-surrender and boundless confidence in God's unfailing love. What causes God pain is our sins and their painful psychological consequences for us. God suffers because we are suffering.

If Jesus has taken away the sins of the world, these are not our fundamental problem. Their consequences, however, are. If there is any sin that offends God, it is our lack of trust in the love of God for us and the fear of divine punishment. The primary disposition and spiritual practice for humans is "to let God love us" (Thomas Hand, S.J.).

11

---◆---

REFLECTIONS ON THE UNKNOWABLE

A COMMON BONDING TAKES PLACE in all who are attracted to the transformative process. Such is the ultimate lineage of all spiritual lineages emerging in the various religious traditions. We are partners/companions in the search, moved by a common perspective and inspiration. Inklings of the contemplative dimension of life are reflected in the world's religions. Seekers resonate to the sound of sheer silence that is provided by the opening of the inner eye of faith. Monastics move towards the Unknowable by witnessing to it in a common lifestyle of complete dedication. The common bond of seekers is to become like a calm lake that reflects the blue sky, in which all the ripples have merged into the surface of the lake as a whole. The lake can then reflect the blue sky, which is boundless in every direction—height, length, depth, and breadth.

Awakening to the contemplative dimension of life is a better term than *discovering*, which suggests searching outside ourselves for what is already present within.

Transformation is not just a positive change in behavior, still less a call to absorb unquestioningly the moral values of a particular culture or religion. It is a change in consciousness in which one sees reality in a wholly new and expanded way. All one's relationships are illuminated by this light. One sees the good in everyone, the oneness of everything, and the wisdom of the divine creative and redemptive plan.

More than an apostle, teacher, or preacher, our vocation as human beings is to be transmitters of divine life. Transmission is not just the communicating of a teaching or message, but *the communication of life* in its evolving sense of opening more and more to the reception of the Ultimate Reality. It is a new perspective on the life we have known and carved out for ourselves as our self-consciousness developed chronologically. It is a new depth of self-knowledge rooted in a more profound experience of love. Saint John of the Cross calls it "the science of love."

There is also a sublime movement beyond union where two kinds of divine life become clear: the created and uncreated, the manifest and un-manifest. Both are available to every human being, even though most of us are still unconscious of it.

Contemplation hastens the evolution of the human species. Whoever finds this out and practices it will hasten the evolutionary future of the human family.

Neuroscience is showing that contemplation modifies the brain in healthy ways. The contemplative dimension of human nature is the innate capacity of human beings to relate to God on the level of union and unity.

Christian tradition holds that contemplation is a pure gift. But it must be emphasized that it is a gift that has *already been given*. Its powers are present but hidden in the unconscious. Hence, we have to be awakened to them. To guide us to this awareness is the purpose and primary duty of religion.

The Judeo-Christian tradition proclaims its vision to love God with our whole heart, mind, soul, and strength, and affirms its mission to love our neighbor as ourselves. These commandments cannot normally be fully obeyed and fulfilled without the awakening of the contemplative capacity buried under the debris of the false self and egoic projects, which are prompted by self-love rather than the love of God.

The contemplative dimension of life includes both prayer and action. For a Christian, contemplation is prayer and fosters a relationship with God that gradually but continuously unfolds as long as we continue to practice.

Historical cosmologies no longer communicate spiritual realities adequately in the light of the geological and biological discoveries of contemporary science. The world religions have to adapt and integrate the new cosmology that is daily unfolding, as well as the new discoveries of sciences such as biophysics, microbiology, anthropology, psychology, neuroscience, astronomy, quantum mechanics, and the new physics.

Contemplation is a gift we have already received. *Waking up* to it is a good metaphor because one wakes up from sleep to whatever one's level of consciousness normally is.

The highest experience of God is no experience. It just *is*. We no longer see the face of Christ because we have in some way become that face. Or more exactly, Christ has become our particular form: "You have died, and your life is hidden with Christ in God" (Colossians 3:3).

12

BLESSING

If one has not received the blessing of one's father, especially in the case of sons, it is hard to pass on a blessing to one's own children or to others. A distant or absent father does not know how to bestow blessings. Blessings were important in the Hebrew culture: Abraham, Isaac, and Jacob all gave special blessings, thus handing on God's original blessing to them.

What if those who are blessed do not or cannot receive it? What happens when the intended blessing is refused or rejected? What do you do with the pain?

Jesus took away the sins of the world and their consequences. What does he do with rejection and the lack of reconciliation? He *identifies* with the agony and pain of those who reject him. He makes the pain of the one who refuses or is incapable of being healed, his own.

What is not transmuted in any conflict situation is handed back in kind, as in the saying of the Hebrew Bible, "an eye for eye, and a tooth for a tooth" (Exodus 21:24).

Thomas Aquinas wrote: "The soul is a certain capacity for God." The soul then is called to participate in the divine nature. In traditional Catholic theology this is called *sanctifying grace.*

Every human being has always been in the mind of God, eternally loved and called to be his child by belonging to the divine–human family (the mystical body of Christ). We were conceived in the mind of the Father in view of Christ's redeeming sacrifice and actualized at our human conception and birth. Our capacity for God can continue to grow forever in the knowledge of God and ourselves (as Saint Gregory of Nyssa taught in the fourth century).

We are God without being numerically the same as God. We are equal to God through grace, without being identified with God by nature.

God is completely wrapped up in each individual human being and their relationships with the rest of creation, especially with other people—that is, with the mission and role of building up the whole human family into the mystical body of Christ in all its fullness. Fear has to be transformed into pure love. At the same time, every possible situation has to happen in order to reveal the full extent of the infinite mercy and humility of God. This includes not just fear and anxiety, but even the experience of terror and horror and, above all, the triumph of grace over sin through its transformation into pure love.

13

WHAT DOES
ACCOUNTABILITY MEAN?

THE PHYSICAL ASPECTS of an act alone do not constitute sin. It is the motive and clarity of our intent that determines the degree of personal responsibility. Thus, physical acts of passion have to be looked at in the context of a person's whole life. These acts can have minimal responsibility (or none at all) depending on the emotional intensity that often reduces or takes away the capacity of our reasoning faculty to choose.

Grave sin, according to Catholic moral theology, has to be fully consented to by the will in virtue of the clear knowledge of the sinful nature of a particular act. Only God can judge these factors. Habit, an obsessive-compulsive personality, tension due to the afflictive emotions, and addictions can make fully deliberate sin almost impossible. The obligation to amend, if there is one in these cases, is to get help if this is possible (spiritual direction, psychological treatment, group therapy, and perhaps all three).

Cultural conditioning and religious education are significant factors in the development of a mature conscience. Discernment is a long process. Emotional factors from upbringing, personality traits, and social influences hinder freedom of choice. Overdependence on childhood and societal mind sets (unquestioned assumptions) have similar effects. It is often necessary for young people to question and re-evaluate cultural influences and parental mandates in order to assume full personal responsibility for their behavior.

Since the eighteenth century, the heresy of Jansenism spread through Europe and the English-speaking countries by people fleeing the French Revolution. Jansenism taught that not everyone would be saved and that only an elite few would get to heaven. The body was considered an enemy and had to be forced into submission by extreme penances and the avoidance of pleasure, relaxation, or even needed rest. God was represented as a severe judge, sending people to hell for an eternity of physical pain, spiritual torment, and rejection by God for failure to keep the commandments.

Christianity in this view became a religion of fear, even for those who habitually strove to do God's will and to serve others at great cost to themselves. Jansenism's strict demands for austerity of life and the practice of severe bodily asceticism became a source of naïve admiration for many sincere seekers. Its influence affects Christian piety even today. Although condemned as a heresy by the Church, Jansenism's rigid teachings have psychologically wounded generations of its adherents and the whole Christian community, and the damage lingers into our own time.

14

THE TREASURE OF
SPIRITUAL POVERTY

"I F AT FIRST you don't succeed, try and try again" is a famous adage for beginners in the practice of virtue. What happens when you give up trying? You finally make friends with failure.

To give in to temptation is to support the ego and the separate-self sense.

The interior rest that humility brings is the immense energy of surrender without seeking any satisfaction or consolation. It is just *to be* and to accept the nothingness of un-manifest reality.

"Blessed are the poor in spirit" (Matthew 5:3) means blessed are they who recognize their absolute dependence and need for God.

The pure love of God is the epitome of mindfulness and heartfulness combined. Interior silence and stillness without movement within or without, effortless yet totally present, constitute the unifying point between rest and activity, at which they interpenetrate and become one.

What attracts God is our spiritual poverty. The essence of salvation is not so much a moral issue as a question of offering oneself completely to God. As Saint Thérèse of Lisieux put it, "We must cultivate God by caresses, that is, by little sacrifices," e.g. letting go of efforts at self-justification, needless criticism of others, and refusing to judge anyone.

We also have to accept being un-evolved in many aspects of our present human condition. God proposes to effect our complete transformation into interior freedom by sharing the divine life with us.

15

IS SCRIPTURE TO BE TAKEN LITERALLY?

WISDOM TEACHERS SOMETIME exaggerate to get our attention and to open minds to the truth they wish to impart. Jesus' seemingly harsh sayings can't be taken literally since they sometimes contradict one of the Ten Commandments and the norm of morality. In the writings of Thomas Aquinas, human nature looked at adequately in all its parts and in its three basic relationships—submission to God, equality with other humans, and stewardship of non-rational creation—is that norm.

Scripture can't be properly understood without contemplative prayer. We are at a moment in time when the tide of divine life from deep within the Trinity is slowly but surely entering the panorama of human history. The Contemplative Outreach organization is simply a wave bringing the movement of divine love into humanity and pushing it further and further onto the shore of time and space till all is submerged in God's being, presence, and boundless love. No doubt other waves are breaking on the shore of time and space and pushing the overflowing tide of divine love deeper and deeper into human experience. Contemplative Outreach is surfing one of these giant waves in order to be cast up as far as possible onto the far-reaching edge of divine love manifesting in ordinary time.

There is only one absolute truth and that is God. There is only one good, as Jesus declared: "No one is good but God alone" (Mark 10:18). We believe that scripture is inspired by God, but that does not mean that God agrees with everything that is said there. We must face the criticism that literary scholars have leveled regarding the various books of scripture. For one thing, some of the meaning of the texts has been lost in translation. The King James Version of the bible, much of its text beautifully rendered in English by William Tyndale (1490–1536), is full of errors in regard to the literal meaning of the text. Other translations are too literal or too broad in trying to interpret the meaning of texts. The actual authors of many scriptural texts are not clearly known. As a result, neither is their intent. Some passages are deliberately allegorical and their pastoral purpose obscures the original words of Jesus. The influence of local mind sets along with cultural conditioning abounds throughout the bible. God inspired the scriptural writers where they were in their cultural and spiritual development. In the Psalms, for instance, some passages reflect a very primitive religious morality and insight; others reveal a sublime relationship with God.

Contemplation is essential for understanding the deeper meaning of scripture. Scripture should be read on a regular basis as *lectio divina* with great dependence on the Spirit, who breathes through the sacred text.

To give to scripture an absolute authority and the final moral voice in everything is a form of idolatry. It is to worship words rather than the God who inspired them.

16

HOW ARE THE SACRAMENTS RELATED TO THE TRANSFORMATIVE PROCESS?

T HE SACRAMENTS MIGHT be related to the transformative process in three ways:

I. *There is an other* is the experience of inner conversion. It is activated by Baptism or major enlightenment experiences resulting in total commitment to the transformative process.

II. *To become the other* is to imitate Christ and is symbolized by the reception of the Eucharist. For denominations or religions without a Eucharist, contemplative prayer may effect the same communion. Both usually take time, normally one's whole life.

Stages of this process have been identified by the Perennial Philosophy, as articulated by the writer Aldous Huxley (1894–1963) and philosopher Ken Wilber (b. 1949), and in the Christian tradition by Saint John of the Cross (*Dark Nights* and *Living Flame of Love*), Saint Teresa of Avila (*Interior Castle*), and others. To combine the daily Eucharist and contemplative prayer which cultivates interior silence and union with the Divine Indwelling is a holistic program for spiritual evolution.

III.   *There is no other* as a stage of consciousness is symbolized by the sacrament of Confirmation, which communicates the Spirit and fully activates the ontological reality of the divine presence and action within. On this level of consciousness there is only the divine manifesting in every creature and the one Self. The identity of the creature remains along with its created capacities, but they have become completely integrated and made whole. Prayer and action are one. Rest and action are one. Everything is in God and God is in them. Everything manifests in its own created way the goodness of God. The Spirit directs all one's thoughts, words, and actions. The emotions are intact and stronger than ever, but no longer dominate or torment the mind. The vast human complexity is simplified. Healthy cells in the mystical body of Christ heal cells that are weak or diseased and build up the organs and bodily systems of the whole organism. One is co-creating and co-redeeming the universe with God.

We have always been in the mind of God and always will be. The present moment is the past and future unified in time and in our consciousness. Thus our process of transformation is carried out not only in chronological time, but also has the timeless quality of eternal life.

All creation and especially intelligent beings are always in God's house (the material creation). They can never leave it. But their awareness of their union and unity with God is meant to become ever clearer.

Evolution (human development) is now focused on humans and higher stages of consciousness (cf. the work of the French philosopher and scientist Pierre Teilhard de Chardin [1881–1955]).

17

———◆———

THE BIRTH OF CONTEMPLATION

CONTEMPLATION MAY ARISE from reflection and affective engagement with a sacred text. In monastic *lectio divina* the text may drop away into pure awareness and one just listens to the sound of sheer silence, which is no sound, just presence. There remains the attitude of listening: alertness without effort. This kind of contemplation is completely receptive. But it is not just passive. It is an affective kind of receptivity, a peaceful and sometimes delightful *being with* the silence, presence, or stillness. This is prayer in secret (Matthew 6:6). The one who prays in this way doesn't think of praying. Actually, the Spirit is praying in him or her. There are no words, no thoughts, just pure awareness with perhaps the sense of loving or being loved, and the longing for oneness.

Theologically, this is to be a *thou* that God calls into

being. Or more exactly, it is to be a *thou* in whom the Eternal Word is returning to the Father: a *thou* that the Son of God is always surrendering to the Father.

Contemplation may arise from a sacred word, breath, glance, or from the spiritual sense of hearing, seeing, smelling, tasting, and touching. One's physical makeup may incline a meditator to one, several, or all of these, but one of them is likely to prevail for a certain period of time:

1. Auditory people: deep listening, cultivating "the sound of sheer silence" (1 Kings 19:12).

2. Visual people: a quick interior glance or general loving attentiveness to God; the light of faith arising from one's inmost being and opening to God's presence.

3. Tactile people: feeling the divine presence descending from above, rising from deep within, or surrounding one as in an embrace or a kiss (The Song of Solomon 1:2).

4. Tasting people: inhaling the Spirit into the depths of one's being; awakening to the Divine Indwelling as boundless, pervasive, all inclusive. Then exhaling this breath of the Spirit, which is divine love, into all creation; into people waiting to come alive, but battered and beaten up by the dusts of this world and unable to help themselves.

5. People of smell: attraction to solitude (to be alone

with God) and to interior silence as to a delicious scent.

Prayer in secret is a term applicable to all of the spiritual senses. It is to be a *thou* in whom and through whom the Word of God is returning to the Father—one in whom the whole gamut of the mystery of Christ, the divine human being, is renewed and manifested. As incarnations of the Son of God, we allow God to experience what it is like to be human in each of us.

18

DOES GOD PLAY GAMES?

THOSE WHOM GOD most loves he often makes most grievous to themselves and to others.

God's love is beyond love as we know it. In the case of Jesus, the Word made flesh was made sin—that is, the opposite of the Father's goodness. To be made sin is to be identified with sinful humanity. It led to the crucifixion and death of Jesus and of his experience of alienation from the Father, which is the natural consequence of sin.

Jesus becomes on the cross the rejection of the one whom the Father most loves and who most loves him. His dying is the surrender of his life out of a love greater than love itself, a gift for which there is no name. In this emptying, Christ in a real sense ceases to be God, and yet manifests that he is the true and eternal Son of the Father. What remains? Only the reality of THAT WHICH IS.

In the Christian tradition this is Christ: Christ, the Word of God not only in Jesus of Nazareth, but in each human being.

Is life as serious as it looks or feels like much of the time? Or is it more a game in which God invites us to take part in a playful spirit? Sometimes, we seem to be winning; at other times, we seem to have lost everything. God at times embraces us tenderly, and a little later seems to reject us. At times, God may seem both close and far away, one of the players in the game, or the referee. In the latter case, only he knows what the score is, and he usually prefers to keep it a secret.

God created everything good—perfect in fact—and continues to do so each nanosecond of time. Sin is not a problem for him. The Father sent his Son to take away the sin of the world. However, the natural consequences of free choice remain, and some of our choices can cause immense suffering. Our suffering is his suffering. One purpose of the game is to learn to endure suffering as the other side of love. This is to know God in his infinite compassion at the deepest possible level.

If we can suffer without suffering, we are not experiencing the true cross. Jesus suffered in agony of body, soul, and spirit. That is the true cross.

The beloved Son of the Father, the Father's perfect image, became the opposite of the Father in his passion and death. Mary of Bethany, in anointing Jesus with the perfumed oil of great price, manifested her understanding and experience of his death and descent into hell. Jesus calls upon his disciples to remember her deed (Matthew 26:6–13), since the whole human family is called like her to join in his burial (symbol of his descent into the psychological hell of our false selves). This is the process of the healing of human limitations and of our transformation into the fullest possible participation in Christ's divine nature.

There is only one I AM. Every human being is a *thou*, called out of nothingness to be I AM, too. We are incarnations of the Word manifesting the I AM of the Eternal Word in our uniqueness together with all the other cells forming the whole Christ, his mystical body. Our personal sense of "me" is an illusion and usually fouls up God's plans in one way or another. When we can let go of self-conscious thoughts and experiences, Christ will be our I AM: living, praying, suffering, dying, rising, and leading us into the bosom of the Father.

Divine love enters into every kind of alienation and embraces it. It heals by loving and sharing love.

Everything just as God made it is perfect, marvelous, indescribably beautiful, good, true, and lovable. We are created to perceive it and to allow it to become always more wonderful. The *mysterium tremendum et fascinans*, explored by German theologian Rudolf Otto (1869–1937), is "to know nothing among you except Christ, and him crucified" (1 Corinthians 2:2). The false self creates our own personalized hell. This is the sin of the world that Christ made his own. The true self, who we really are, is created in the image and likeness of God. Our true nature is God manifesting God-self in us.

God is more mother than father, especially in the cultural conditions in which the scriptures were written.

Why be surprised or paralyzed by the feeling of emptiness, inability to remember God, or to make acts of love, gratitude, and surrender?

Just *to be*, at certain times, may include the feeling of spiritual destitution. It may involve the bombardment of temptations that seem endless and impossible to resist, and that are often accompanied by the fear of entertaining them and thus committing sin. Spiritual destitution may be the experience of failure and the powerlessness to do anything to feel the presence or empowerment of God. This state is either what is meant by hell in the book of Revelation, or is something worse that is as yet unnamed. It is more painful than the feeling of nothingness. Perhaps it is what is meant by the state of consciousness that Saint John the Baptist called "the sin of the world" (John 1:29). This was the suffering that Jesus was sent to take away. We are invited to participate in his healing activity by suffering for the whole mystical body of Christ, which may at times involve the experience of acting contrary to our conscience.

The Blessed Mother has taken responsibility for every

human being, past, present, and to come, through her identification with Jesus and his redemptive work. Like him, she too was made sin for our sakes. She invites us to join her in the same experience.

There is no other when you have become the other, and the other is you. It is compassion: one and yet distinct from everything. The Ultimate Reality is the capacity for infinite relationship. In this becoming, everything comes into being. Only Ultimate Reality matters, and for that very reason everything matters.

If one creature experiences enlightenment, everything in the cosmos moves toward enlightenment.

For God's sake, we must be willing to be surprised, to start over from scratch, to expect and love adventure. We must venture into the unknown and into all that liberates. In other words, we must be willing to forget everything, to learn everything, to be anything, or nothing. Above all, we must serve God's love and plan for the new creation.

God wills to play games, to try things, to create new things and new situations. In light of this, we need to be prepared to be known or unknown, to please others or to be despised. We need to be ready to be lonely, or extremely socialized, to be well or to be sick, to live or to die.

God's adventurous spirit is manifest, especially in the Eucharist. There, God offers himself as food and drink (his body and blood, soul and divinity) to anyone who comes to the table, even though everyone is free to reject him.

God is who we are, more than we are. In and with Jesus, God calls us to union and unity with the Father by giving us his Spirit, thus enabling us to share in the divine generativity. We are both creatures and children of God. "Blessed is the one who comes in the name of the Lord" (Psalm 118:26) means that God, who is always here, is always coming in each precious moment together with its content. In this sense, past and future are present in the experience of now.

God's math is infinitely detailed and infinitely diverse. God likes to be free to do anything; and he wills to give us this same freedom. He is free to be you, me, or to be anybody; to be nothing, or a material creature. He is free to love and free not to love at the same time.

Whatever God knows *is.* As cells in the body of Christ (all creation) we are created with his sacred humanity and always being created in him and with him. The past and future are now. Time and space are our perception of reality as evolving beings, not who we really are. We are co-creating everything with Christ as we evolve as individuals and as a species.

19

GAME TIME

ARE WE SIMPLY God's thoughts, and is this whole evolving universe from the Big Bang on in fact an illusion? In some ways, it seems to be a marvelous video game, full of extreme violence and ecstatic moments. Did Shakespeare have this kind of insight in mind when he put on the lips of Jacques, one of his most memorable characters, "All the world's a stage,/And all the men and women merely players" (*As You Like It*, II.vii.139–140)? Could it be that what we are experiencing is just an illusion or the most elaborate dream ever? The popularity of video games, in which people are more and more involved, is a striking example of this idea.

If our lives are games and part of the grand game of the evolving universe, then as thoughts in God's mind we must exist forever in God's eternal consciousness. The separate-self sense is only a thought that does not exist outside of our particular consciousness. If we let that thought go, we will be where we always were, which is in God's thoughts. In this sense, there is no death except for the false self, the ego, and the separate-self sense, all of which create and sustain the illusion of separateness.

"Whoever believes," Jesus said, "has eternal life" (John 6:47). Hence, they cannot die. The dissolution of the body as we know it is only part of the illusion of the separate self. Even in this life, in the most tumultuous of situations, we cannot be separated from God, because we are eternally encompassed and immersed in his intimate generativity and creativity. This insight might enable us to be happy no matter what happens in the video material of our physical lives, because we know that we are always in God's house, which has no boundaries. The *thought* of a separate self is all that separates us from God. The horror, fear, and alienation of acting against our conscience make up the hell we create for ourselves. Liberation from this suffering is what the concept of salvation, redemption, and holistic healing really means.

20

WHAT IS CENTERING PRAYER?

THE SABBATH REST was imposed by God because it is necessary for *us*. Resting and listening feed into each other. Resting means, above all, rest from compulsive activity, mixed motives, and emotional excesses.

Pure love is the rest of interior freedom; it is our participation in the divine life. Matthew 6:6 describes what is called centering prayer, an invitation to participate with Christ in the life of the Father.

Centering prayer is not a rejection of other forms of prayer. Rather, it points to a further level of relationship and intimacy with God.

Centering prayer is like *hearing the music rather than just the notes*. Beyond all the noises of our mind is the mysterious "sound" of silence, which is no sound. The sound of no sound takes place when deep listening morphs into Presence.

Centering prayer is not free of thoughts, but grows with daily practice in detachment from them. It is to will to be totally present to God "mouth to mouth," the physical symbol of heart to heart, which emphasizes the intimacy and intensity of the prayer relationship.

Centering prayer is an invitation to the furthest possibility of human nature, which is to become divine. Not however like Adam and Eve, who wanted to become God *on their own terms*. God wants us to become God too, but *on his terms*, because these are the only ones that work.

Jesus' invitation is to become "no thing", i.e., not attached or over-identified with anything. We are to become detached even from our *idea of God*.

Steps of centering prayer:

- Letting go of the external environment
- Letting go of the internal environment, i.e., thoughts and all internal movements
- Letting go of self-consciousness

Too much effort at letting go, however, is itself a vestige of the false self.

God's word spoken at creation set off a resonance that continues to vibrate throughout the universe and in us.

The consciousness into which we move through pure prayer (contemplation) is Christ Consciousness.

We share in centering prayer when done in common a reservoir of silence that is enhanced by each one's contribution.

Prayer in secret is letting go of expectations and desires, "and your Father who sees in secret will reward you" (Matthew 6:6). The Aramaic word for *reward* might be paraphrased in this way: "Your Father will cause your whole human nature to blossom, bloom, flourish, become whole, and be transformed."

Engaging in this prayer is not so much *doing* nothing as *being* nothing. The willingness to let go of our false self is the work of the Spirit within us.

Silence is the greatest teacher there is. God's creative Word is uttered in sheer silence, and it is our ability to resonate with it that furthers our transformation. We can't get "there" by ourselves. So we consent to God's doing "it" in us. We can't climb the ladder of transformation, but we have the innate capacity to receive it.

Just as a healthy cell in the human body can heal or replace dying cells, so we can bring peace, healing, and wholeness to other cells in Christ's mystical body.

The kingdom of God is actually a state of consciousness, but not just any state of consciousness. *It is Christ's consciousness of the Father as Abba (Daddy).* Christ's humanity is the most sublime manifestation of the Trinity.

Creation can be seen as the womb of God who is always nourishing and preparing us for eternal life. Death is the birth canal to eternal life.

The healing of centering prayer is not limited to physical healing; it goes to the root of our problems, the emotional programs for happiness. Centering prayer gradually undermines those programs through the Gift of Knowledge, which impresses upon us the reality that only God can satisfy our boundless desire for happiness. This leads into the night of sense as described by Saint John of the Cross in "The Dark Night of the Soul." God is letting us in on the secret of our weakness, not as a judge, but as the most intimate kind of sharing between friends.

Daily life tests the sincerity and authenticity of our spiritual journey. We are brought to a peaceful contentment with the faults that we cannot overcome: cf. Saint Paul's thorn in the flesh (2 Corinthians 12:7). Saint Paul ends up boasting of his infirmities.

The spiritual journey fosters an ever-increasing trust in God's loving care and in his total identification with us in all the events of our lives.

21

HOW DOES CENTERING PRAYER CULTIVATE THE LOVE OF GOD?

CENTERING PRAYER IS bigger than Contemplative Outreach, which is a way of cultivating and supporting it. Centering prayer provides practices for introducing, sustaining, and encouraging insight into a process that might be called the Christian lineage and which transmits that experience from generation to generation.

What is the motive or source of the transmission of divine light, life, and love? It is the infinite mercy of God—the Trinitarian self-giving that knows no bounds—stooping to identify with our spiritual destitution.

To consent to be a creature enables us to be freed of our limitations, to be united to God, and to co-create the universe.

The crucifixion and death of Jesus is God's invitation to

be transformed in Christ. To be transformed in Christ is to cease to have the limitations of creaturehood.

Christ has identified with the human condition by becoming one with us in his incarnation and death: "For our sake [the Father] made him to be sin who knew no sin" (2 Corinthians 5:21). If we are willing to identify with Christ made sin, we will rise with him to eternal life and oneness with the Father.

Our sins are not the problem, because Christ has taken them all away. Sin is the state of being a creature, not God; we are imperfect by nature.

The reality we call God in the Christian tradition is protecting us and using our negative activity with all its consequences for our liberation and transformation into the life of the Trinity.

If we let the sense of our nothingness, spiritual destitution, and powerlessness penetrate our consciousness through and through, we can be deified as completely as the Word was made flesh in the incarnation.

The inner experience of being suspended over the abyss or void without any support or hope of support is a short cut to the experience of the new creation. Creation and the void are not just a plan. They are happening all the time.

Nothing trivial is unimportant, and what is important is insignificant in the light of THAT WHICH IS. The Ultimate Reality is manifesting infinite goodness, compassion, tenderness, and humility in every nanosecond of time. God has two ways to accomplish this: forgiving the endless evil we do, or removing in advance the temptations that might lead us to sin (Saint Thérèse of Lisieux).

How to be "a certain capacity for God" (as Saint Thomas Aquinas puts it)? Perhaps the answer is: to be a capacity *with nothing in it!* This is to love everything and at the same time to be ready to give up everything at a moment's notice.

But does God's plan have any takers? It is the path to perfect love, but beyond anything we know or can imagine as perfect love. It is surrender as pure receptivity, spaciousness, and the experience of time from the perspective of eternity. "To fall into the hands of the Living God" (Hebrews 10:31) is the safest place in all of creation!

To accept the humiliation of being a creature is the only way to participate fully in the divine life. The hands of God, according to scripture, are tender, welcoming, soothing, caressing. But something in us desperately wants to be God *on our own terms* and secretly resents being created. This is pride, the unwillingness *to forgive ourselves for not being God*. This unwillingness makes it difficult to accept the totally gratuitous gift of God-self.

Perhaps the most difficult aspect of the divine reality for us to accept is God's humility—his willingness *not* to be God. That is the opposite of our orientation, with its implicit desire, however unconscious, to resist God's will and to be God on our own terms.

Each human person manifests God's infinite humility, God's willingness not to be God. This involves a love that transcends love itself as we conceive it, the sacrifice of what we most love (ourselves) for the sake of a still greater love.

We must offer ourselves to God just as we are, not something else. We must offer ourselves to God just as he is, and not some idea of him.

22

IS GOD ALWAYS PRESENT?

MOMENTS OF AWARENESS of the divine goodness can become every moment. God is always present: always at rest and always active at the same time.

To say, "I am unworthy of God's love," is not a true statement. More accurate would be, "Although God created me with inconceivable beauty, I have made myself unworthy."

At the same time, gratitude is infinitely more important than the feeling of unworthiness. If we fully acknowledged our created beauty and the godlike gift of human intelligence, we might be less likely to tarnish that glory by forgetfulness of God and our indifference to his presence.

If Christ lives in us, he must pray, speak, act, suffer, and die in us—and rise again.

As regards prayer in secret (Matthew 6:6), it seems to mean:

To be silent: no deliberate thoughts

To be still: no deliberate desires

To be Christ's self: no movement apart from him, whether interior or exterior.

Then it is "no longer I who live, but it is Christ who lives in me" (Galatians 2:20).

The *mysterium tremendum et fascinans* is consciousness without self-consciousness.

A human person seems to be a certain orderly arrangement of reality conceived as invisible energies. The Creator God is that which is beyond reality.

The term *hypocrite* comes from the word *actor (hypokrisis)* in Greek. Thus a hypocrite pretends to be something he is not. If we try to get off the stage, where can we go? The seats are filled with people just like us, who have false selves, too. Where can we go to find our true selves or to be who we really are? Such is the human condition. The only resolution is that God must take over our lives completely.

23

———————◆———————

WHY CULTIVATE INTERIOR SILENCE?

WHY GO INTO solitude and silence in so thorough a manner as an intensive or prolonged retreat?

The answer, I presume, is to experience the deepest silence. Is this kind of retreat a form of self-pleasuring on the spiritual level? Or is it an experience of just *to be*, opening uninterruptedly to God's presence and to the enormous energy of love that creates and sustains us and the entire cosmos?

Silence is to become nothing, to enter the void (the world of no creation). This is to pray to the Father and to relate to the secrecy of the Ultimate Mystery. The purpose of such a retreat is to sink into the invincible conviction of being loved by God, loved simply because one has become aware of one's own desperate need and of one's complete dependence on God.

God chose Saint Paul to be the prime revealer of his

love for the non-Jewish world of his time, perhaps because he was one of the chief persecutors of Christians and had rejected Jesus. In this way, the humility of the Father is revealed. The wounds we inflict on his beloved Son, which are made visible on the cross, become Saint Teresa's "fountains of pure love": "I have come to call not the righteous but sinners to repentance" (Luke 5:32).

Redemption is not only restoration of lost innocence and the forgiving of all sin. It is the transformation of people and sin itself with all its consequences into unconditional love.

"Behold this heart which has so loved people," Jesus reportedly said to the French mystic Margaret Mary Alocoque (1647–1690) during her vision of the Sacred Heart surrounded by a ring of thorns.

Jesus was made sin for our sake (2 Corinthians 5:21) so that he could manifest the humility of the Father. We have lost the enjoyment of the image in which we were created or, from an evolutionary perspective, we are on the way to experiencing it—or both. These are two perspectives of the same reality. We are to become truly free, or rather Freedom itself. To evolve into that state as permanent is our destiny. It is the plan of God hidden from eternity and revealed in Christ Jesus.

Both the bible and genuine science are revelations of the creator God as the process of evolution continues its movement through time.

24

TO BE COMPLETELY TAKEN OVER BY GOD

GOD'S PLAN: to manifest divine humility and infinite compassion and to make each human being his equal to the maximum degree possible, transformed into divine love. To please God, all anything has to be is itself!

Everything about God is wonderful but completely beyond articulation. The experience of God beyond thinking is all experience at once and much more. God is always a surprise, intimate beyond belief, more personal than we are to ourselves. We suddenly understand what real life is. Any hesitation about the absolute goodness of creation ceases. It is the integration of every level of human experience and of the "peace of God, which surpasses all understanding" (Philippians 4:7). It is more than divine union. It is to be a capacity for God that is always expanding, always broader, higher, deeper, and more exquisite.

The gratuity of God's presence, with its infinite variety and diversity, is endless joy. To be infinitely loved by God as a personal experience is to be liberated from all the limitations of creaturehood and to be united to THAT WHICH IS. Unity consciousness is to let God act through us at every moment without resistance.

God is manifesting in each moment as the human consciousness in each of us. As the Canadian Jesuit Bernard Lonergan (1904–1984) said, "We are the icons of God." God experiences himself in us and awakens his dispositions in us, especially humility, forgiveness, and compassion. God receives his own love from us in the Spirit and delights in sharing with us the Trinitarian life of total self-giving.

Is not the transformation of human beings into God-self the supreme act of divine omnipotence and perhaps God's greatest glory?

We experience God within us through dispositions that surpass in generosity and knowledge anything that we can do or imagine of ourselves.

God looks for experiencers more than theorists. In our culture we tend to want to be the latter and to avoid the former, especially when life is painful. Thinking is normally a lot easier than being. It is our predominant cultural conditioning in a time of rapidly developing technological skills and massive scientific information. The cybernetic age is primarily about information, not experience, understanding, and love. These spiritual values need to be infused into it.

Christ lives in us. This is our answer to every question, experience, or discovery. We are called out of nothingness to work at this. It is the Father's will. Nothing can change it. It is our true reality. *Christ lives in us* means that he prays, acts, thinks, loves, suffers, and dies in us; and at the deepest level *is our true Self.*

God needs experiencers rather than thinkers (theorists) in order to know what it is to be fully human. Our precious days on earth—the spiritual journey—are not primarily about us, or even about our transformation in Christ. They are about *God taking over our lives in every detail.*

To repeat the same insight slightly differently, living daily life and the evolution of consciousness are not primarily about "us." They are about God and God's life, death, and resurrection in us. They are about whatever God wants to do or doesn't want to do. They are not about our past or future or even about our present circumstances. For Christ to be "us"—to take over every aspect of our life in space and time and to experience our human existence in this present moment—that's what the latter days of life are aimed at. The goal is not just union, or even unity with God, but God *incarnating in our humanity with all its circumstances.* Christ renewing the sacred mysteries of his human life in our humanity is one way of describing his incarnation in each of us.

Purification is an up-and-down movement of consciousness: the scrubbing, so to speak, of the soul between these two actions. It is also the healing and completing of our creation out of nothing: to be taken over body, soul, and spirit by the Eternal Word of God; to be an extension of Jesus in space and time; and to contribute to the continuation of the ongoing evolution of the human family.

A certain radiance and interior glow may accompany divine insight and even energize the body at times. One knows one is being lived in by God. One is bound to feel lonely and deprived when that sense of the divine presence passes or diminishes. But each crisis leads to a deeper sense and conviction of divine union.

To sacrifice divine union we must first have it. Then comes the experience of the desert, the passion, and death of the Word of God in us, and ultimately our descent with Christ into hell as a psychological state for the salvation and transformation of the whole human family. Hell is a psychological state more than a place. It is the state of experiencing the consequences of deliberate sin, the chief characteristic of which is the anguish of alienation from God.

Formation for the transformative process—the ultimate purpose of human life—consists not in some perfection of our own, but in the growing awareness of being created out of nothing.

To be nothing is to be totally receptive to God's love and totally honest regarding our faults. As Saint Thérèse of Lisieux wrote, "Only one thing really matters: to work solely for God and to do nothing for self or [to please] creatures."

25

THE TRANSFORMING
FIRE OF DIVINE LOVE

CHRIST IN HIS incarnation united himself to the whole human family, assuming human nature into his divine person and giving each of us the capacity to be united to the Father through him and in him. Christ is one with us according to nature and desires to make us one with the Father by introducing us into the intimate life of the Trinity. Then Christ and God, as Saint Paul teaches, will be "all in all" (1 Corinthians 15:28).

God wants us to enjoy him not only in the state of transforming union, but to make each of us equal to him in every way that is possible. Though remaining ontologically distinct, we are to become existentially one with the Trinity. Did not Jesus pray for this grace for the human family in his last discourse (John 17:21)?

In the book of Revelation, it is written, "[Christ's] feet

were like burnished bronze, refined as in a furnace" (1:15). Perhaps we could say that his body was baked by the Spirit until it was transformed into pure spirit, and then transformed again into the glorified body of the only begotten Son of God.

We, too, through grace are being made into an offering to the Father completely consumed in the divine fire of the Spirit communicated to us by Christ's passion, death, and resurrection. We, too, are being smelted by the divine fire dwelling within us into participators in the divine nature.

To practice centering prayer is to descend into the furnace of divine love. Christ turns up the thermostat to burn away our undue attachments to life in this world and to ourselves. This is the implication of Saint Thérèse of Lisieux's act of oblation, offering herself to infinite, merciful love of God as a victim. She begs God "to consume me unceasingly, letting flow into my soul the floods of infinite tenderness which are contained in Thee, so that I may become a martyr of thy Love."

The heart (understood as the inmost center of our being) contains the Spirit as a living flame of love. In "The Living Flame of Love," Saint John of the Cross addresses the Spirit in these words: "How tenderly you wound me in my inmost being!"

We enter contemplative prayer to access this flame and to allow it to intensify. It can be consoling, "coolness in the burning heat" as the hymn *Veni Sancte Spiritus* puts it. Or it can be like the unbearable heat of a blast furnace. It can be purgatory or a foretaste of heaven, depending on the will of the Spirit, who responds in a divine way to our particular and personal needs. It gradually becomes a continuous flame, as on a gas burner, always ready to burst into high at the touch of the Spirit. Our faults, like uncooked seeds, are consumed in the fire of divine love.

We carry this flame into everyday life, where it transforms our intentions and actions into the appropriate response to the *now* of each passing moment, until the Father and his beloved Son, Jesus Christ, become "all in all" in us.

Thus our bodies become one with and within Christ's glorified body—one flame of infinite love expressed in the immense diversity of individual flames smelted into one gigantic fire. As Saint Paul writes, "You have died, and your life is hidden with Christ in God" (Colossians 3:3). This text refers to the grace of the Ascension, which is perfect oneness with God. We no longer live as individuals, but in the words of Saint Augustine, as "one Christ loving himself" (Homily 10 on the First Epistle of John). Or to put it another way: God in us loving God in everyone else.

Compassion is to be, and even feel ourselves to be, the mother of everyone in the human family.

26

IS THE UNIVERSE A REVELATION OF GOD?

THE UNIVERSE SEEMS to be a giant paradigm of the spiritual journey. Thanks to the discoveries of astrophysics and associated sciences, it is possible to see the stages of human development reflected in the Big Bang, the endless expansion of the universe, and the birth and death of nebulae, galaxies, stars, and planets. Black holes and supernovas are expressions in matter of the spiritual qualities of the intelligent material beings that we are or are becoming. The evolutionary process is going on at every level of existence and must affect us in some way that we do not understand as yet on planet earth. Does the changeless One learn from the created universe and intelligent beings by becoming one with us?

The supernova and its final dissolution by exploding and sending forth into space what remains of its nuclear energy—its very substance—is a symbol of the ultimate death of the ego and the birth of unity consciousness. The star literally collapses upon itself and gives away all that it has or is, blasting its enormous energies across vast reaches of space and, eventually, becoming myriads of new galaxies, stars, and planets in the expanding universe. Thus, the dying star co-creates the universe of matter with all its potentialities—perhaps even life itself—together with the Creator.

Christ is the ultimate supernova in this metaphor. He literally pours himself out—"empties himself"—and becomes nothing in order to become everything. On the cross, he invites his followers to do the same: to enter fully into the death and resurrection of the evolving universe. This supreme sacrifice is expressed in each of us in varying degrees according to our destiny or vocation.

Saint John of the Cross's dark night of spirit (and the still deeper night of self) is a spiritual paradigm of the collapse of a supernova upon itself.

On the human level, this process of death and resurrection may feel like losing one's mind. One is confronted and overwhelmed by the *mysterium tremendum* without always feeling the balancing reassurance of *et fascinans*, the irresistible attraction to union and unity with God. The dying may be sheer terror, powerlessness, and apparent annihilation of the individual self, without any possible escape or place to hide. One feels at times ripped apart, squashed, paralyzed, indifferent to living or dying.

This experience is to identify with the crucifixion of Jesus and to die more completely than in physical death. Its completion is the moment of resurrection (redemption). It is the release of divine energy capable of transmitting the divine light, life, and love, and of raising up new communities of seekers and lovers of God. It challenges societies on every level, but with great gentleness, compassion, and kindness, creating means of healing for every human need. Like Jesus after his resurrection, we may work on earth or work from heaven to heal humanity's immense wounds. Or we may continue Christ's return to the Father through the grace of the Ascension.

If God has chosen us for some particular work, nothing can prevent him from accomplishing it, not even our sinfulness and bungling.

What Jesus is doing and suffering in his passion is what the Father is doing eternally: manifesting love beyond love. All sacrifices are contained or hidden in this one, the sacrifice of Isaac expanded to infinity.

27

---◆---

IS THERE A NIGHT OF SELF?

To be without consolation, especially spiritual, is a call to expose oneself to a relationship with the God who is un-manifest. It is a state of consciousness beyond transforming union, which is union with created grace and the revelation of God as Creator. Saint Thérèse of Lisieux seems to have experienced union with uncreated grace during the last year of her life. Perhaps the dissolution of her fragile health hastened or deepened her spiritual suffering, including her growing sense of complete powerlessness. In her last year and a half of life, none of the truths of faith had any attraction for her anymore. Both God's love for her and her love for God were unfelt. It was a passage through hell understood as the absence of the sense of God's presence and even existence. She knew she was suffering for the whole human family and sharing in Christ's living and dying process at every level of her being. Her temptations against faith, she said, were uninterrupted.

Her long trial, as she described it, sounds more intense than the night of spirit as described by Saint John of the Cross. Perhaps it might be called the night of self. In any case, every thought of herself was painful, full of doubt and uncertainty. At times she felt rejected and abandoned by God. She was dispossessed of everything in her life that had previously been meaningful and supportive. Consolation on the physical or mental level of her being was completely dried out. She felt her life had no meaning, doubted the value of her inspired Little Way, and distrusted her longtime disposition of boundless confidence in God.

She hesitated to share these temptations with her sisters for fear of scandalizing them. Her former invincible hope in God was buried in dense darkness. She felt she was imprisoned or in a black hole. She heard hissing sounds in her ears, while the words of atheists were repeated over and over in her imagination. Without faith, she wrote, "I would have committed suicide without a moment's hesitation" (*Last Conversation* 22.9.6).

In spite of all this suffering, Saint Thérèse knew she was still called to divine love and to work for the salvation of sinners. She was learning to love beyond all the created graces of the spiritual journey, beyond reliance on anything that had previously supported her on her spiritual journey, and which had led to her total surrender to unconditional love. As she wrote in her autobiography, "In the heart of the Church I shall be love!" became her invincible aspiration and conviction.

Perhaps the full depth of her vocation is only now becoming understood. With the development of evolutionary theology as well as by the new cosmology provided by contemporary science, God may be moving humanity to a more widespread relationship with that aspect of God that might be called the un-manifest. Advaitic Hinduism knew that dimension of divine union centuries ago. Brahman in their view is the un-manifest aspect of Ultimate Reality. The clearest example and embodiment of this consciousness in recent times is the Hindu guru Ramana Maharshi (1879–1950).

The Buddhist teaching of no self also relates to Ultimate Reality or the Absolute in a non-personal way. To relate to God as uncreated—the void of absolute nothingness—if shared by a growing number of people would contribute immensely to the transformation of the human race into the mystical body of Christ and what was anticipated in the early Christian communities as the "new creation."

In Christianity, the *mysterium tremendum et fascinans* may approach this profound insight. Perhaps Saint Thérèse was pioneering for the Christian tradition this understanding in the final months of her profound transformation.

28

THE BEAUTY OF CHAOS

WE TRY SO HARD to put order into our lives and into the cosmos. There is none; instead, there are lots of comings and goings, ups and downs. In fact, everything at the subatomic level is chaos. Moments of perfect order coalesce only to dissolve again into the thrilling immensity of infinite possibilities. Love is all because it is nowhere, not in one place, but *everyplace*. Every form is teeming with life and with various forms of consciousness or no consciousness. Like bees swarming or in a hive, or ants on an anthill, life on every level is busy. Yet it's doing nothing—remaining for a moment and then quickly passing away, only to be back in another form, in another kind of community, in another chaos. Chaos is our home. It is always becoming, ending, and starting anew.

Everything moves but in no particular direction. It just

is; always changing, becoming something new; always together with everything else; dependent and interconnected; differentiating yet always the same; fusing, one-ing, never still; always in relationship to everything. Only love remains.

We are a certain openness to being everything and nothing, both at once and in all that is in-between. This is God in us and we in God. This is eternal life, shared in common with all other creatures in an infinite variety of ways.

Nothing really matters because everything matters and is happening at the same time. Nothing is remembered or forgotten. It is all here at once. Everything is in movement, going nowhere but enjoying everywhere and everything. This is creation: endless, delightful, unpredictable, unbelievable; just *is*-ness and *is*-ing playing with goodness, beauty, and truth; without purpose, without plan, without judgment; in perfect peace in the midst of activity and no activity.

To be in a relationship is to accept everything and to resist nothing. It welcomes enemies and makes them the best of friends, whether they be people, angels, demons, problems, difficulties, pain, suffering, or desolation. All is in the void, which is the safest place in all creation, where gratitude, freedom, and pure love reign supreme.

29

THE MYSTERY
OF THE TRINITY

CENTERING PRAYER COMES out of the life of God moving within us. We may first experience this movement as a longing for something more, a wordless desire for union with something or someone beyond ourselves. Moments of union may have come to us in the form of the sacred in nature, listening to great music, or observing the stars on a clear night. This longing may be more defined by our religious practices like meditation, the prayerful reading of scripture, receiving the sacraments, or various devotional practices.

Centering prayer activates an existential relationship with Christ as one way of receiving the fullness of unconditional love pouring out of the depths of the Trinity into creation. As we sit in centering prayer, we are connecting with that immense flow of divine life within us. It is as if our spiritual will turned on a switch, and the current (the divine life) that is present in our organism starts to flow. It is waiting to be activated: "On the last day of the festival, the great day, while Jesus was standing there, he cried out, 'Let anyone who is thirsty come to me, and let the one who believes in me drink. As the scripture has said, "Out of the believer's heart shall flow rivers of living water."' Now he said this about the Spirit, which believers in him were to receive" (John 7:37–39). Jesus, of course, is referring to the experience of what might be called the contemplative dimension of the Gospel or, more exactly, the contemplative dimension of life.

The source of centering prayer is the Trinity, the divine life within us, begun in baptism or whenever we receive the state of grace. The doctrine of the Divine Indwelling of the Trinity is the most important of all the principles of the spiritual life. It means that God's own *life* is being communicated to us, even though it is beyond the level of our ordinary faculties because of what might be called, to use a modern scientific analogy, its high frequency. It is so high in fact that only pure faith can access the divine presence in its full actuality.

The doctrine of the Trinity affirms three relationships in the one God whom tradition calls the Father, the Son, and the Holy Spirit. This is the principal mystery of the Christian faith and the source of all the others.

"Father" in this context encompasses every human relationship that is beautiful, good, and true, but it especially evokes the sense of parenting or "sourcing." The doctrine of the Trinity has been developed in many different theological models over the centuries. Drawing on these models, we can affirm that the Father is the ground of all potentiality. The actualization of that potentiality within the Trinity is the Word—the Father coming to full expression of all that the Father is. In a sense, the Father is nothing until he speaks the Word. He knows who he is only in the Son, who is his interior Word or consciousness.

The Spirit is the common bond of love that flows between the Father and the Son in total self-giving love. In other words, the emptying of the Father, the actualization of all that is contained in infinite potentiality, is expressed totally in the Eternal Word within the Trinity. The Father pours himself into the Son. One might almost say that there is nothing left of the Father. The traditional theological teaching affirms that the Father lives in the Son, not in himself.

The Son, in turn, confronting this immense goodness that has been handed over to him, returns all that he has received to the Father in a kind of embrace, or what some Fathers of the Church called "the most sweet kiss of the Father and the Son." The Spirit is the love of the Father and the Son, their common heart. In the Trinity, there is no self, no possessive attitude. Everything is self-surrender. Everything is gift. Everything is love. As Saint John the

Evangelist affirms unconditionally, "God is love" (1 John 4:8).

All creation comes into being in and through the Word. Thus, the Word is the creative source of everything that exists (as the prologue to Saint John's Gospel avers), expressing itself in different ways throughout the various levels of creation. Creation consists of unlimited manifestations of infinite reality without in any way exhausting that reality.

The emptying of the Word in becoming incarnate is the expression of what the Father is doing all the time in expressing his interior Word. Accordingly, when the manifestation takes place in creation, it has to be expressed by some form of emptying. Divine love, when it enters creation, has to suffer, because there is no way in which that love can be fully expressed in created terms without the Father in some sense dying. In creating, God ceases to be God; at least, God ceases to be God in the way he was before creation. God becomes totally involved in creation because each creature expresses something of the beauty, goodness, and truth of the Eternal Word, the absolute fullness of God's expression.

Jesus Christ is the human manifestation of this extraordinary love. This is the heart of the Christian mystery—mystery, not in the sense of an intellectual puzzle, but in the sense of wonder and awe, communicating a delight that is inexpressible and that demands, as the only adequate response, our total surrender in return. The Trinitarian relationships, of their very nature, invite us into the stream of divine love that is unconditional and totally self-surrendered. This boundless love emerges from the Father into the Son, and through the Son is communicated by the Spirit to all creation. The invitation is given to every human being to enter into the stream of divine love, or at least to venture a big toe into the everflowing river of eternal life. As we let go of our false self, we move into this stream of love that is always flowing and bestowing endless gifts of grace. The more we open our capacity to receive, the more we can give. And as we give, we enlarge the space in us to receive still more.

30

POWERLESSNESS

My grace is sufficient for you, for power is made perfect in weakness.

— 2 CORINTHIANS 12:9

POWERLESSNESS IS OUR greatest treasure. Don't try to get rid of it. Everything in us wants to get rid of it. "Grace is sufficient for you," but not something you can understand. To be in too big a hurry to get over our difficulties is a mistake because we don't know how valuable they are from God's perspective. Without them we might never be transformed as deeply and as thoroughly. If everything else fails, the dying process is the place where we will have no choice but to go through the transformation process because everything is in fact taken away.

The spiritual journey is the commitment to allow everything we possess to be taken away *before* the dying process begins. This makes us of enormous value to ourselves and to others because we have anticipated death, and death is not the end but the beginning of the fullness of transformation. If we were born, we've already been through a facsimile of death and our body is well prepared for the final translation, or transition as some prefer to call it. We can't see God without going through death because the intensity of his naked presence would burn us up and turn us into a grease spot.

Jesus Christ in his lifetime had to hide the dignity and power of his divine nature. A constant miracle was required to hide the enormous radiance and power of his inner nature. The one time it appears is at the Transfiguration when his face shone and his clothes became whiter than snow. That was the only occasion the glory of his divine nature was allowed to come through.

Christ is choosing the lowest place all the time, the very lowest place. Why? Because that is what God does. God is not attached to being God. He doesn't care about praise or thanksgiving. What he is interested in is our consent to his love of us.

Saint Paul was transformed by God's communication of Godself to him, and so he writes, "I will boast all the more gladly of my weaknesses, so that the power of Christ may dwell in me. Therefore I am content with weaknesses" (2 Corinthians 12:9–10). That is the disposition of transformation. Transformation is not about great spiritual experiences but coming to terms with our own human weakness as we experience it. Saint Paul then lists his other difficulties, "insults, hardships, persecutions, and calamities for the sake of Christ, for whenever I am weak, then I am strong." When we understand that, we don't need any more education.

When we feel that we're suspended on top of nothing and are not grounded anywhere; when we're confused, have no place to go, and feel God is far away; that we are separated from God, or even that we are alienated from God, we have been given the dispositions that arise in the dark nights through God's immense love. These are the ways that our human nature is conditioned little by little and at a pace that is appropriate for each one's needs, vocation, personality, and limitations. It is so well thought-out that we can't even put it in a category; it's the most expert and profound form of psychotherapy.

God knows us through and through and still loves us infinitely. Although we are being sustained on the physiological level, biophysics tells us that the body itself has to evolve in certain ways to sustain intelligence, and then to sustain divine communications. We are not ready to receive the enormous reality of God without preparation in which all the elements of our human nature collaborate. God is working with the obstacles in us with extraordinary gentleness, tenderness, firmness, and patience. If you want to know yourself, talk to God. He knows.

Finally, powerlessness is the greatest power there is

because it enables one to simply be more and more a channel of God's power and love.

What do we really want to be at this point in our spiritual journey? Have we set our goal on becoming a saint? The main problem with wanting to become a saint is that it is a desire that *isn't good enough*. One is settling for a kind of second-rate identity. Suppose we are culturally drawn to the Asian religious traditions and want nirvana, enlightenment, or the wisdom of some great guru. No matter how we see the goal, it is the dark night that is transforming because it is in the dark night that we become powerless. With time we become content with our weakness and happy to be utterly dependent on God.

Now we are in the first step of the Twelve Step program of Alcoholics Anonymous, which is probably the most brilliant synopsis of the Christian spiritual journey there is. What is the first step? "We became aware that our lives [through whatever the addiction is] had become unmanageable." That is, we can't do anything with it. This is the perfect disposition for transformation. The dark nights bring you there; that is their job. By doing so, although it is a little uncomfortable, it is a lot easier than the inconveniences of being an addict of some kind. This plunge into the abyss of God's goodness reduces our only possession to the infinite mercy of God. But what more do we need? There isn't anything greater.

Jesus is recorded in Matthew 10:39 as saying, in effect,

"If you want to save your life [accomplish all the things the false self is interested in] you'll bring yourself to ruin. But anyone who brings himself [or herself] to nothing will find out who he [she] is."* And who is that? *Everything.* Nothing is not nothing but *no thing*, no identity outside of God. By becoming no particular object, we become what God is, which is no particular object, but everything. This is a totally non-possessive attitude toward oneself.

Jesus taught that to be his disciple we need to deny our "inmost self." That is more crucial than the other things he invites us to separate from. Any identity at all, apart from God, is not *it*. To have no identity or the identity that God wants us to be is what the transformative process is designed to bring about. To want to be anything other than God is not humility. It does not give due credit to God's generosity since he wills to give us not only everything, but his very Self.

* New American Bible *The Vatican II Weekday Missal for Monday of the 15th week in Ordinary time.* Copyright 1970 by the Confraternity of Christian Doctrine, Washington, D.C.

31

EPIPHANY—THE FEAST
OF CONTEMPLATIVES

A Homily

EPIPHANY IS THE FEAST of contemplatives in all the world religions and in humanity.* We can't escape the invitation to become a contemplative because all we have to do to receive it is to be born and I presume we have all experienced that. At the culmination of the Christmas season is the feast of the Epiphany. Epiphany means revelation. What revelation? Each of us is manifesting God, or at least we have the potential of doing so along with every other creature. . . . But there is more. The feast of Epiphany reveals that God is inviting us to participate in the union of the Son of God with human nature. The incarna-

---

* Cf. *The Mystery of Christ*, Thomas Keating: 1: The Christ-Epiphany Mystery.

tion of the Word made flesh is the marriage between the divine and human nature in Jesus Christ. We share in the mystery of the Word made flesh in virtue of the oneness of the human species and become one body with Christ. This revelation is symbolized in the Gospel text by the water changed into wine. In this image we humans are the water and the Spirit is the wine.

Epiphany is the Christian celebration of what our brothers and sisters in the other religions call *enlightenment.* Enlightenment is the inward realization and consciousness of being identified with who we really are. We are not our false selves or egos. Kiss them goodbye. They have no future. We have to have an ego in some degree to function in this life, but the most important aspect of our life is the revelation of God that is going on all the time in the details of life. We know that a subatomic particle is in relation to the wave from which it comes, and that we are localized expressions or manifestations of the wave of divine energy from which we come. We call our wave *God*, which is a kind of nickname because there is no word for this primordial wave. It just is, is, is—IS-ING without any limitation at all. If we have an existence at all, we must be present to and penetrated by this presence.

Why not cultivate it? That is the invitation of Epiphany. Why not become unified or identified with God so that we manifest God in every action, and in this way give God a chance to find out what it is like to be a human being. That seems to be the project. But it is only half the project. The bigger half is the effort God has been making since the beginning of time to convince us that he loves us. We are pretty shy about that; not too good candidates for divine love at that level, which is the meaning and source of every other love: physical, mental, and spiritual.

The Church has great courage, and perhaps even a little presumption, in celebrating Epiphany the way she does: that is to say, the revelation of God on three distinct levels—the remote, the proximate, and the actual. In other words, there are levels of understanding, penetration, and realization in the feast and its significance that the liturgy is trying to communicate.

The coming of the Magi (first level) is the remote call of all humanity to union with God. Divine union is an invitation to everything that ever existed or will exist. The baptism of Jesus (second level) is the proximate call of a certain group of religious people, the Jews, to a more intimate communion with the source of all that is.

The Marriage Feast of Cana (John 2:1–11) is the crown of the Christmas/Epiphany season (third level), which in this context is the celebration of the marriage between God and humanity. We need a little subtlety to penetrate its full significance. What is being revealed in this wedding feast? What is being revealed is that the Divine Nature has united with our human nature and that this is becoming conscious in the lives of ordinary folks like us.

Epiphany is also the celebration of God's nuptials with specific individuals, that is, with you and me. That is why I call it *the feast of contemplatives*. Contemplation is the process of human enlightenment that goes on over the years. Old age is the time to do nothing in order to be more and more taken over in body, soul, and spirit by this incredible love that is always with us, but has to be uncovered by a certain amount of discipline, by the trials of life, and by trust and self-surrender to the immediate presence of God. God is sheer compassion, forgiveness, tenderness, and in certain situations, playfulness.

This is the love we are invited into on this feast day under the symbolism of a marriage feast. Please notice the circumstances. The wine has run out. In those days people celebrated marriages for three or four days. The mother of Jesus observes the problem but doesn't ask for anything. She has already got everything so she doesn't have to ask for anything. But at the same time she is concerned for everybody else's needs, especially this couple who will be embarrassed when the wine actually runs out. So she said to Jesus, "They don't have any wine." God is sensitive and eager to fulfill our every want and need, though sometimes withholding or delaying granting what we want in order to move us to a deeper level of trust and intimacy.

Everything that God does is coming from love with an immense energy that science is just beginning to suspect. Invisible energies have to become felt or sensed for us to understand them. In this instance, Jesus uses the senses. He is reluctant to start his ministry ahead of schedule by what would be a miraculous event. You will observe that Mary didn't ask him for a miracle. She just presented him with the problem, giving him credit that he might figure out what the best solution might be, something we don't always do.

There were six jugs holding about 180 gallons of water sitting there. Water is the most pervasive element on this earth and there is plenty of it. Notice that in many miracles and in so much of the divine action, it is abundance and the incredible limitlessness of the gifts of God that are emphasized.

Here Jesus is changing six jugs of water not just into more water, but into something different, more exhilarating, healing, life giving, exciting, even intoxicating. An enormous amount of water is changed into wine, enough to serve a small army, or provide for about twenty or thirty other weddings. Nothing picayune about God! What he gives is limitless. It is not wrong but sort of unenlightened to ask God for particular things, although that is sometimes part of the Spirit's inspiration. When you can have everything, ask for everything! Ask for everything because it is the totality of the divine life that is being offered.

The changing of water into wine is the total transformation of water. As necessary as it is for life, water is not usually favored as the proper liquid for celebrations. People like something a little more delightful. Wine is the sign of God's delight in giving Godself to us. Perhaps you noticed in the first reading the striking sentence from Isaiah (62:5) that God delights in giving himself to us in the same way as a bridegroom marrying a virgin. In other words, his relationship to us is sexual as well as spiritual. Every divine reality that God can communicate to us is contained in the Eucharist. He is giving himself away totally and having a great time doing it.

If you've been a happy bridegroom at some point in your life, you can sympathize with this disposition. What joy God may have given you as you anticipated your wedding night is what he feels about each one of us right now, and God is encouraging us to celebrate that invitation and above all to receive it. The sacraments of the Church are about the transmission of divine life and love. They are about the interpenetration of spirits; they are about the symbols and beauty of sexual love raised to the level of total gift of self.

To be a contemplative is to be willing to be loved concretely in every detail of life and on every level of human life, body, soul, and spirit. If you are merely thinking of receiving the Eucharist as a ritual, go home. That's not what it is. It may start with that, but the Eucharist is primarily about the interpenetration of spirits—all that we are into all that God is, and all that God is into all that we are, including every detail of our life, every concern, joy, and suffering. In other words, we've got a life companion of infinite capabilities all lined up in our favor and ready to go.

Why be afraid of anything? We've got the greatest gift of the cosmos, the friendship of God, and he wants to celebrate even if we may be a bit tired this morning.

How do we celebrate? Gratitude, self-surrender, enjoyment of the divine presence—these are the dispositions that make us a contemplative. The experience of God's presence and action within us leads to a greater and greater capacity to see this action in everybody else and throughout the cosmos. It creates a marvelous open-mindedness toward all truth. God then has the freedom to enrich us as he wills and as he has planned in incredible detail.

One last thought. The new wine provided by Jesus at the marriage feast was obviously to be consumed, so it was meant to be nourishment. It was meant to be digested. It was meant to affect the nervous system and the brain and to enliven the dispositions of all the guests.

Divine love has no conditions. We are invited into it not as an abstract idea or as a ritual only, but as an experience. Contemplation is the experience of God that is becoming continuous and permanent even in the details of everyday life and amid the distractions of computers and the ghastly reports of the horrors of violence throughout the world. The divine goodness and the presence of divine love are always there. As our contemplative clarity deepens, we move from the occasional experience of the Presence to a permanent state of loving interaction on a moment by moment basis.

In the season of Epiphany, we should put aside all fear and surrender to the Eucharistic presence in which Christ, that is God, gobbles us up. If you are a passionate lover, you know that sometimes your love for the other is so great it wants to eat the beloved up. You want to consume the beloved and to be so united you can't ever be separated. This is how God feels toward us. The Eucharist is changing us. This is what transformation or enlightenment really is. Our human personality, capabilities, faults, even our sins are being consumed and transformed into divine life by this extraordinary transformative process. This is what we call in the Christian tradition *the process of contemplation.*

So be yummy! That is to say, really surrender to God! Turn your life over completely to love and see what remains— hopefully nothing but God. So let God be all in all in you. Let him be the bridegroom whose desire for communion with us gives him such delight. This is the revelation that confirmed the faith of the apostles. The marriage feast of Cana is God's symbol of the transforming intention of the divine will in our lives. This feast of divine light is not the end of the journey but the beginning, in which we begin to see and live with the enlightened eye of faith. We live then not just with the Other, but as the Other and gradually *become* the Other. Eventually *there is no Other* because we have become the Other, too.

Contemplation is the process of Christian transformation (enlightenment in the Asian religions). The Marriage Feast of Cana symbolizes the initiation of the transformative process: water transformed into wine; the human into the divine; flesh into Spirit.

APPENDIX

The Process of Centering Prayer and Its Corresponding Dispositions

Disposition of Meditator (attitude)	Centering Prayer (practice)
1. Acceptance	External silence: entering the inner room
2. Consent	Interior silence: silencing the interior dialogue
3. Surrender	Prayer in secret: contemplation
4. Pure Awareness	Stillness: motionless within and without
5. Solidarity	Oneness with God and all creation
6. Cosmic consciousness	Consciousness without particular content
7. Union of action and contemplation	Union with God both in prayer and action
8. Total surrender	Unity consciousness: death of the separate-self sense (non-duality)

The Passage through Consciousness

The innocence of childhood, ego development, transformation of consciousness, and recovery of the divine innocence are all necessary stages in the evolutionary process leading to conscious unity with God, the realization of who we really are.

ABOUT CONTEMPLATIVE OUTREACH

Contemplative Outreach is a spiritual network of individuals and small-faith communities committed to living the contemplative dimension of the Gospel. The common desire for Divine transformation, primarily expressed through a commitment to a daily centering prayer practice, unites its international, interdenominational community.

Today Contemplative Outreach annually serves over 40,000 people; supports over 120 active contemplative chapters in 39 countries; supports over 800 prayer groups; teaches over 15,000 people the practice of Centering Prayer and other contemplative practices through locally hosted workshops; and provides training and resources to local chapters and volunteers. Contemplative Outreach also publishes and distributes the teachings of Fr. Thomas Keating and other resources that support the contemplative life.

For more information about Contemplative Outreach, visit www.contemplativeoutreach.org.

ABOUT THE PUBLISHER

LANTERN BOOKS was founded in 1999 on the principle of living with a greater depth and commitment to the preservation of the natural world. In addition to publishing books on animal advocacy, vegetarianism, religion, and environmentalism, Lantern is dedicated to printing books in the U.S. on recycled paper and saving resources in day-to-day operations. Lantern is honored to be a recipient of the highest standard in environmentally responsible publishing from the Green Press Initiative.